Through the Door

Imagine if you walk
into your new school,
a bit wary,
maybe a bit anxious,
and a magic door
suddenly appears...

Written by
Y7 students of the
Vision Academy Learning Trust
2023

Published in paperback in 2023 by Sixth Element Publishing
on behalf of Vision Academy Learning Trust

Sixth Element Publishing
Arthur Robinson House
13-14 The Green
Billingham TS23 1EU
www.6epublishing.net

© Vision Academy Learning Trust 2023

ISBN 978-1-914170-43-0

British Library Cataloguing in Publication Data. A catalogue record for this book is available from the British Library.

All rights reserved. No part of this publication may be reproduced, stored in a retrieval system or transmitted, in any form or by any means, electronic, mechanical, photocopying, recording and/or otherwise without the prior written permission of the publishers. This book may not be lent, resold, hired out or disposed of by way of trade in any form, binding or cover other than that in which it is published without the prior written consent of the publishers.

The authors assert the moral right to be identified
as the authors of this work.

This is a work of fiction. Names, characters, businesses, places, events and incidents are either the products of the author's imagination or used in a fictitious manner. Any resemblance to actual persons, living or dead, or actual events and places is purely coincidental.

CONTENTS

Introduction 1

Part I 5
Egglescliffe School, Stockton On Tees

A Jump Through Time by Betsy Blackburn 7
The Test by Ruben Farnell 19
Making Friends by Molly Gamon 33
Dark Dimensions by Charles Hind 43
Cleo Overcomes Her Fears
by Nicola Hatton 57
The Invasion by George Sapstead 67
Conflict by Matheew Swift 73
The Beauty Of Being Different
by Rosie Turnbull 79

Part II 91
Huntcliff School, Saltburn

Imaginary by Sophie Allan 93
The Mystery Elevator by Isaac Basham 97
Ghost Story by Brooklyn Coonan 103
The Clown Chase by Amaya Cooper 107
The Mysterious Door by Ruby Donaghy 113
The City Of Clues by Alexxa Hutchinson 117
The Boy by Jayden Leader 125
The Reality by Eva-Rose Maynard 129
Hero by Kadee-Lee Philips 133
The Magical Door by Esmerelda R 139

Part III 143
Laurence Jackson School, Guisborough

The Puzzle by Jeff Bails 145
The School Lockdown by Jaiden Bousfield 149
The Mysterious Beach by Emily Coe 153
Into The Light by Leoni Dixon 167
The Mysterious Storm by H.J. Hakin 177
The School Mystery by Summer Loftus 183
The Flower by Tulisa Lowe 189
Verdun! by Oliver Morris 195
Becoming Mio by Kai Watson 203

INTRODUCTION

I have always found that stories – the writing and the reading of them - possess a magic ability to teach and foster reflection and self-belief in a way that feels like leisure rather than industry. Co-ordinating this project has certainly made me see things from a different perspective and I hope it offers the same to our readers.

This writing project came into being one rainy afternoon, as Gillie Hatton and I sat down to ponder how we could help the students in our Trust to reflect and find a confident voice. We talked about how the transition to secondary school could be a daunting one and thought that an anthology of stories aimed to help new Y7 students who, for a variety of reasons, might need a bit of help getting 'Through the Door' would provide an excellent focus. The achievement of our student authors is a gift to those who read their stories – we should all aspire to their tenacity, commitment and dedication.

Vision Academy Learning Trust as a community has made this project possible and I would like to thank everyone who has contributed: Mr White, our CEO for placing such value on reading and Literacy and making a commitment to inclusion and high expectations for all. Thank you to our school librarians, Mrs Walmsley and Miss Barker for their expertise and patient coaching of our young authors. We are grateful to the staff who have typed drafts, given feedback and encouragement: Mr Powell, Ms Longstaff, Ms Ferens, Mrs Crawford and Mrs Nowell.

Finally, thank you to Gillie Hatton without whom none of this would have been possible. I hope with this project we have opened the 'door' to many more collaborations, bringing stories and hope to the young people in our Trust.

Jo Parnell
Lead Practitioner for Literacy,
Vision Academy Learning Trust

Egglescliffe School, Stockton on Tees

A JUMP THROUGH TIME

Betsy Blackburn

You've done it again! You are completely lost! Well done, Aadya! The sounds of the children in other classrooms filled the brightly lit corridor as I walked for what felt like hours. Clattering dramatically, the raindrops thundered down onto the windows, racing each other all the way down. I clung to my heavy backpack as I feared it may fall off, and turning the corner, I spotted a sign that read 'Welcome to the English corridor!'. I'd made it! Finally!

I approached the rusting spruce wood door hiding behind the bookcase, the door that should lead to my English classroom. I opened it and stepped through…

But it wasn't my English classroom.

As my eyes adjusted to the shimmering sun, I looked around my surroundings and was instantly drawn to the towering maple tree. The ground around it was charred, embers and ash scattered around its base. Looking closer, I spotted that there were large logs hung at the bottom, with a circular pole sticking out through the middle. My attention changed as I examined the rural surroundings of the village, I was in.

People were walking all over the place, many entering their tiny straw houses. The men were dressed in smart leather tunics, falling just below their knees. The women, however, were wearing plainly coloured long dresses, made out of coarse material.

A woman began to approach me, her ginger hair falling just below her shoulders and her green eyes shimmering.

"Aadya," she began.

I panicked. How did this woman know my name? I didn't know who she was.

"Y-yes?" I responded, stuttering on my words.

"It's okay," she replied. "I know of you and require your help."

"My help? Are you sure that I am the right person?" I said.

"Yes. I am certain. Now follow me."

I didn't know what to do. I needed to go back. "I... No, I need to go back through the door."

"Aadya, It's okay." She reached for my hand and I pulled it close and held it in my other arm. "Please, Aadya," she said. "You are the only one who could help." After seeing the uneasy look on my face, she added, "Trust me. I do not want to hurt you. Please."

I gave in. This woman seemed so kind. She only needed help and then I could go back through the door. I hoped it wouldn't take long, though. I had to get to my class soon.

The woman led me through trees that towered over our heads like umbrellas.

"I need you to help keep me safe," she said at last.

After a silence that lasted an age, I finally decided how to respond.

"How am I supposed to do that?" I said, unsure of exactly what she was asking of me.

"You need to stay here and help me convince my neighbour to spare my life. She thinks that I'm a witch."

Another silence filled the air. How was I supposed to do that when I had a class to go to? What would I do if my parents were worried? What if I got stuck here? What if I died? What if I couldn't help her?

But did that really matter? I need to help this innocent young woman. I couldn't just do nothing and let her die, could I? I had made my decision.

I took a deep breath and said, "Okay, I will help you as long as I can still get back to my life. I don't want to stay here forever."

"Thank you!" the woman said. "I promise you won't regret it!"

It took me a while to respond to this.

"It's okay, but, if you don't mind me asking, what is your name and how did you know mine?"

The woman turned away and quietly said, "My name is Molly and yours, Aadya, is written on your nametag."

"Oh," I said, feeling stupid. "Okay."

"First of all, we need to get you some new clothes. You need to blend in," Molly said.

"But what about my li-" I said, being cut off.

"Don't worry about that, dear," she said. "We will keep them locked away in a cabinet. We need to make sure nobody gets suspicious. Now, go change into your linen dress, and make sure people do not spot your old clothes."

I promised her I would and snuck round into a closed area of the hut. After changing into my new white dress, I took my clothes to Molly and she tucked them away out of sight.

"We need to come up with a reason I am here," I stated.

"Good idea!" she said "If anybody asks, you are my niece and staying with me."

"Okay..." I responded, quietly.

Later that evening, I sat at the dinner table with Molly, talking about what we were going to do.

"So," I said, "who is accusing you of being a witch?"

Molly looked up from the speck of dirt she was staring at. "My neighbour, Miss Bane," she said at last. "She promised to accuse me as soon as the witch hunters came back to town as they are doing other trials at the moment."

I took a minute to think.

"Okay," I said, realising what we could do. "We could try to find a way to stop her from doing that before the witch hunters get back."

"That's a great idea, Aadya," Molly said. "We just need to come up with a way to do that."

I gave Molly a small nod of agreement and began to wonder how we were going to do that.

Suddenly, I realised that I didn't know why she was being accused.

"Molly…" I began slowly, "why are you being accused of being a witch?"

Molly turned her head to meet my gaze, her green eyes staring into mine.

"Well," she began, "around one month ago, a black cat visited me. He looked like a stray so I took him in and gave him food. Eventually, my neighbour, Miss Bane, saw me with a black cat and said that she would report me to the witch finder general..." She trailed off and we both turned our gaze away.

"Oh..." was all I could manage, thoughts rushing through my mind faster than I had time to acknowledge them. What if I got caught trying to save Molly? What if I died? What if my parents never knew what happened to me?

I took a breath, gathering all my thoughts together, then I eventually said. "What happened to the cat?"

Molly sighed before saying, "I let him go into the wild so they wouldn't find him and he would be safe."

I looked down, nervously, hoping that this would all work. I went to bed shortly after, my rush of thoughts eventually lulling me to sleep.

The next day, Molly decided to take me on a walk while we thought about what our next move would be and so I could learn the local area and map out where everything was. While we were walking, we heard screams.

They were quiet at first and then got louder and louder until I spotted something struggling in the river.

Or rather, someone.

"Molly, look over there! What's that thing?"

Molly followed where my finger was pointing and looked stunned.

"I think that 'thing' is a child, Aadya," she said, still staring into the river at the struggling figure.

"We need to save them!" I exclaimed, already getting ready to run.

Molly nodded her head and said, "Yes, follow me."

And then we ran as fast as we could, down the hill towards the river, being careful not to trip and fall in.

By the time we got to the riverbank, I was out of breath.

Molly leaned down, pressing her hand into the ground and spoke to the child.

"Are you okay?" she said.

The child looked at her with helpless eyes and moved a mop of curly brown hair out of their face. Looking closer, I realised that it was a boy.

"I am going to help you, okay?" Molly lowered her right hand down into the river, keeping the left one on the ground for support.

The boy flinched but took her hand and she helped pull him up.

He rested on the soft grass, struggling to breath.

"Are you okay?" Molly asked. "What happened?"

The boy didn't reply until he slowed his breathing and then said, "I'm okay, I fell in the river while I was walking."

Molly gave him a reassuring smile. "Okay then. Do you have a name?"

The boy thought for a second, looking unsure if he could trust them but then said, "My name is William."

Molly thought for a second and then said, "Okay, William, do you have any family? A house?"

William, again looking unsure, replied with, "Yes…"

"Would you like us to walk you home?"

William took a second to reply, turned away but then mumbled, "Yes, please."

William led the way mostly, but Molly and I stayed close behind. After about ten minutes of walking, we eventually arrived at William's house. Molly looked shocked and gave me a look that made me realise that William was Molly's neighbour! At that moment, William's mum came out of her house, examining her child.

Molly mouthed something to me, that looked a lot like, "That's Miss Bane." Eventually, Miss Banes turned to her son and said, "William, what did this awful woman do to you? You're all wet."

William took a breath before saying, "They saved me. I fell in the river."

Miss Banes' face dropped and she turned to Molly. "You? You saved my child?"

Molly nodded.

"I… Thank you," she mumbled. "I

suppose you're not a witch after all. Now, please leave my home."

I could tell that Molly was also containing her excitement.

"Are you still going to report me?" Molly said.

Miss Bane mumbled, "No, please leave."

Me and Molly both knew that it was good enough and that Molly was saved.

After returning to the hut, we celebrated and I changed into my school clothes. We gave each other an awkward hug and I said, "Bye Molly."

And she responded with, "Goodbye, Aadya."

I then turned around, looking at the hut one last time and stepped outside.

All that was left for me to do was to locate the door I had come through. I eventually found the door under the same maple tree it had stood under when I had first entered the village. As I opened it, it gave a loud creak of disapproval, as if complaining for me leaving it for so long. Taking a short breath, I opened it and stepped back through the door…

My eyes adjusted to the darkness again, my head spinning with thoughts. For a moment, I didn't recognise where I was. I looked down the corridor and pulled my map out of my pocket. I suddenly realised I had English class. According to my map, my class was just next to here. Walking further up, I eventually found my classroom.

"Hello, Aadya," my teacher, Mrs Bonnet, said. "You are just over there." She pointed to my seat.

"Thank you, Miss," I said, walking to my seat and feeling a lot more confident.

I can do this, I thought. After all, secondary school isn't that bad and, after all I have accomplished, this worksheet doesn't look that hard. I can do this!

THE TEST

Ruben Farnell

1: THE BEGINNING

It was a bright summer's day. The sun was shining, everything seemed normal. The birds were chirping and the air had the smell of freshly cut grass. A boy named Mike was staring at the clock on the classroom wall. In all of his thirteen years of being alive, nothing had seemed to go so slowly. Finally, the bell rang and break began. Then he started his morning routine: get his waffles from the cafeteria and pick on the same scrawny child named Tom.

After his usual beating of slaps, punches and kicks, Tom pleaded, "Why do this? I mean, come on! I'm obviously outmatched! You're a tall strong boy with blue eyes and brown hair while I'm a ginger haired, green eyed, glasses wearing geek! My bones could break from a single trip, I mean I'm one large pump away from death!"

Everyone knew that Thomas Gibson was the biggest nerd in the class, however he was also the most likely to become a billionaire and own a mansion. Maybe they were jealous.

Suddenly, a low buzzing sound descended. Mike and Tom looked at a brick wall with a green door attached to it, which had not been there before.

They took a peek inside, it was a blank room that seemed to go on forever. They decided to go in. Then, a white mist seemed to creep onto the door. When the mist cleared, the door had vanished. Mike and Tom ran frantically to where the door had once stood, utterly bewildered by what they had just seen. Tom started to breathe heavily and mustered enough breath to whisper, "My mum is going to kill me!"

Mike grabbed Tom's shoulders, shaking him and slapping his face side to side, insisting "Pull yourself together!" Deep down, Mike was just as scared, the thuggish persona and bravado that had carried him through his secondary school years until now, starting to crack. Mike turned to Tom. "You must have a plan in that big brain of yours?"

Then Tom realised something. Tom did not know what to do.

All of a sudden, mist started swirling around them. After approximately ten seconds, the mist enveloped them.

2: THE MONSTER

Mike woke up in a cold sweat. After scouting ahead, he realised where he was. He was on a tropical island. After waking Tom up, they decided to walk towards the horizon. After travelling a long time, suddenly bamboo trees rose up and out of the ground and separated them.

Mike shouted, "I need you! I need your brains!"

Tom replied, "You need my brains?! I need your strength!"

Tom then looked to his right. He saw a place where the bamboo trees stopped and where they could meet again.

Tom shouted, "There's an ending! Let's walk on ahead until we get to the clearing."

Whilst they were walking, two ominous forces watched them from either side. Eventually the trees became so dense, they could neither see, nor hear each other. Mike suddenly saw Tom right behind him but something was off. Tom had his chest puffed out and he seemed more confident in himself.

Meanwhile, Tom noticed that Mike was behind him.

"How did you get through?" Tom asked.

'Mike' said blankly, "I found an opening in the trees which I used to slip through."

Tom was confused but both decided not to question.

Meanwhile, on the other side of the trees, Mike was questioning the other 'Tom'.

"On a scale of one to ten, how brave would you say you are?" Mike quizzed.

"I would say a ten," answered 'Tom'.

That's when Mike knew this wasn't the real Tom.

Back on the other side, Tom was secretly investigating the 'Mike' on his side.

"Would you ever say you would bully someone?" Tom questioned.

'Mike' replied with, "I would never. I am the person who would usually get bullied."

"You probably would," Tom agreed. "But… you're NOT the real Mike!"

All of a sudden, the fake Mike pulled a sick grimace that seemed to elongate way beyond his face. He turned grey and scaly until eventually it looked like a second skin, much like a snake.

All of a sudden, a chameleon-like creature leaped at him. Unfortunately, Tom wasn't fast enough. The creature opened its mouth and sprayed webs at Tom. Eventually Tom succumbed to the web-like cocoon. The creature screeched a roar that shook the earth.

Meanwhile on the other side of the trees, the other Tom started shedding his skin.

Mike looked behind him, and before the chameleon had a chance to leap at him, Mike punched him.

The chameleon got back up and swept Mike's legs from under him.

Mike landed on this back and while incapacitated, much like the other chameleon, this one also cocooned Mike in a sea of webs.

All of a sudden on either side of the bamboo trees, the chameleon creatures grew a scorpion's tail with a poison barb at the end. After being stung by the poison barbs, Mike and Tom were consumed by darkness. When they woke up, their cocoons were dangling from the ceiling. Stalactites were surrounding them. It seemed like they were in a cave.

3: THE CAVE

They heard screeching coming from the back of the cave. The loud screeching got the attention of Tom and Mike. Tom whispered, "We've got to get out of here."

"You don't have to ask me twice," replied Mike.

Tom realised something. In his chemistry class they had been talking about a specific type of spider that had very strong webs. These webs also had a very strong chemical reaction to heat. Tom realised they were very close to a hole with sunlight seeping through.

Tom also realised, near to his cocoon, which was the furthest from the light, the ground was covered in large rocks. Each one increasing in size from right to left.

"Alright, I have a plan," Tom explained. "Your cocoon is closest to the sun's rays. And these webs will melt if you swing towards the light. Once you are out of your cocoon, you can climb across the rocks to reach me, then you can swing me with enough momentum to melt me out of my cocoon and set me free. On three… One, Two, Three…!"

For once in his life, Mike listened to Tom. He swung from left to right vigorously. Eventually, the dangling piece of this cocoon snapped and he fell, thankfully not with enough noise to attract the creatures' attention.

"Okay, now free me," Tom sighed with relief.

Now Mike had two options. His first would be to leave Tom, the person he had bullied for years, or he be could be kind, setting him free from the creatures that had captured them. Although, every single part of his mind told him not to, his conscience chose otherwise. With a hop, skip and a leap, literally, he leapt onto the cocoon and swung Tom.

Before they knew it, they were running out of the cave, the monsters all swarming around them and the island swirling with a thick fog.

4: THE FOG

They found themselves transferred to the blank room they had once been in before. Except something was different. It was mistier than previously.

This mist began to take on the form of a lean giant. On the left side of the giant it was a male, and on the right side it was a female. The female side had light skin, while the right side seemed to have a darker shade. At the top of its spine, two necks came out, each one having the same shade as the side it was on.

The left neck sprouted a female with blonde hair. She had a black beauty spot on her cheekbone, whilst on the right neck, there was a male with brown, short cropped hair. Both heads had glowing white eyes and no visible pupils.

Mike, with sickening realisation, recognised his parents in the deformed creature before him.

The male side of the monster bellowed, "You are a huge disappointment to our family! You are the reason shame has been brought on the Peterson name! Before you, our family has won the annual sports fest for decades."

"Wait a minute, the competition to see who is the best at sports by hosting a match of each one. Rugby, cricket, tennis etc?" Tom questioned.

"He was never good at sports," the female part of the giant replied with venom.

All of the sudden the monster shouted out in anger and began beating its fists on the floor, breaking solid stone into dust. They reached over to Mike, grabbing him and tossing him to the ground like he was nothing. The monster's anger was overwhelming. Mike began to be pummelled by the monster. Tom could only look on in horror.

In a sudden burst of rage, Tom used all of his energy to unleash punches to both heads of the giant. It was then Tom realised what was going on.

"I know what these monsters represent! The chameleon monster showed a façade.

A person putting on a fake version of themselves. This monster represents your fears. You fear you're a failure in your parent's eyes. That portal door wasn't meant for both of us. It was only meant for you. If you think about it, it makes sense."

Tom looked thoughtful. Without even realising it, he knew how to get out of their predicament.

"Wait! I think I have a plan!" Tom exclaimed.

"Last time you had a plan, we got dragged back here again," Mike shouted over the thumping of the fists he was trying to dodge.

"Just trust me, please!" Tom pleaded.
Mike nodded.

Tom started whispering to Mike. All of a sudden, Mike ran up the monster's back and into the space between the two necks. Mike made as much noise as he could, the monster's heads screaming in agony. Then Tom, with all of his brain power, conjured a sword out of thin air and stabbed the monster's heart.

Apparently in this world, whatever you imagined could come into being.

All of a sudden, the monster exploded and with that, the white room was empty except for the glowing green door.

The boys rushed to it, arriving back at school.

Miraculously, whilst in the white void, time had not passed.

The bell rang for the next lesson.

"Friends?" Tom questioned.

"Friends!" Mike replied.

They walked off to fourth period with their arms around each other's shoulders, their friendship forged though their trial.

THE EPILOGUE

In the end, Mike sorted his relationship with his parents, Tom got to see his mother once again and eventually, Mike became a PE teacher at the very school he went to as a child. Tom became a billionaire, creating a power source big enough to eradicate climate change and solve world hunger.

They kept in touch, with the events of that day having an everlasting impact on them and creating a bond the likes of which the world had not seen.

Meanwhile, in the same school, another child was bullying a classmate.

All of a sudden, they heard a creaking. Would you believe me if…?

Well, never mind, that is a story for another day.

MAKING FRIENDS

Molly Gamon

1: THE DOOR

5, 4, 3, 2, 1! A shrill, high noise pierced through the classroom's boredom like a sharp dagger. Liv picked up her bag and sprinted out of the maths classroom. A cascade of warm sunlight tumbled down onto her as she stepped outside. School was finished, and she let out a sigh of relief. Today had been the worst day ever.

Pulling a thick spined book from her bag, she wrestled with a terrible monster, longing to escape into one of her books. Suddenly, an ominous shadow cast over her. From nowhere a door appeared. Wooden and ancient, it was suspended in mid-air. Her hand was drawn towards it… she gripped the cold, brass door knob, thrusting it open.

A lush meadow of tall green grass spread

out in front of Liv and the warm radiant beams of sunlight shone down onto her back.

In the distance, she saw a table, so she ran towards it, trying to find some help. Placed on the oak table was a set of ornate silver cutlery and delicate China teacups. Liv thought to herself that something seemed familiar… this was the Madhatter's tea party from one of her favourite books, 'Alice in Wonderland'. Out of nowhere, a fluffy white rabbit appeared in a little striped waist coat.

Liv laughed to herself, "You're the white rabbit!"

The rabbit replied, "And you're Liv but you can't stay here much longer, the storm is following you! It haunts our world, created by all the bad thoughts you ignore and dismiss. We must escape before you are taken!"

From a pocket in the rabbit's waistcoat, he pulled a shiny round watch hanging on a long chain. Before Liv could worry about how she was suddenly inside a book, a rabbit hole popped out of the ground.

"Quick, in here!"

Liv scrambled through the hole with the rabbit into a small room.

"That should hold it up for a bit," shouted the rabbit.

Relieved to have escaped the storm, Liv looked around, disorientated. The rabbit had grabbed a small velvet pouch and after a bit of time, he pulled out a handful of beautiful magic rings, shiny and glimmering.

"These will take us to a new book where we can try to escape. Here, you hold the bag." He tossed one of the rings into the air and it burst into golden dust which settled on the floor to form an ominous, gaping hole. Truthfully, Liv wasn't too sure about this, trusting an imaginary creature from a story. But it was her best chance of escape. So, holding her breath, she jumped in and tumbled down the pitch-black hole.

2: THE QUEEN'S DUNGEON

"Thud!" The sound reverberated around the stygian gloom. Liv stood, and looking around realised she was in a dungeon. The walls were made of icy cold bricks. In front of her there were tall, restricting bars. But where was the rabbit, she wondered? He was gone. Had he abandoned her? Audible footsteps, slow, heeled, deliberate, echoed all around her. The rabbit was the last of her problems.

Raised voices echoed around the subdued dungeon. Liv strained to see the woman who was making such a commotion but when she did, her heart dropped right into her stomach. She was in the Evil Queen's dungeon! And the other raised voice was the magic mirror.

"What do I do?" Liv said under her breath, her voice cold and timid now.

The dungeon was impenetrable and all hope was gone. Liv wondered if she would ever escape.

A deafening cackle broke through Liv's thoughts. The Evil Queen strutted over to her cell. "Who are you?" Her voice made the floor shake.

Liv replied, "I am Liv and I'm stuck so please help me!"

The Queen let out a burst of barbaric laughter and uttered a single word, "No!"

Out of the air she conjured a large pair of keys and selected one with an intricate looking design. Its handle was rusty and tarnished. She pushed it into the cell door and grabbed Liv.

Liv's wrist burned where the Queen held it. Then Liv remembered, the magic rings! As she threw one on the floor, it opened into a swirling purple portal and Liv jumped in.

3: MEETING AN OLD FRIEND

A heavy sigh of relief escaped Liv's lips as a new scene materialised around her, a glittery mist filling in the gaps of the jigsaw.

In front of her stood a figure, a tall, lanky, freckly, red-haired figure from one of Liv's books.

"Hello, I'm Anne Shirley of Green Gables. What can I help you with?" the girl asked.

"Actually, I am looking for a white rabbit who can help me get back home."

"Well, I can help there. I have just met a rabbit and he was heading towards the lake. Come on, I shall take you there!"

When they reached the lake, Liv saw the white rabbit sitting on the edge. He turned around and looked at Liv, his little beady eyes lighting up with joy at the sight of her.

"I thought you were gone forever, and I would never get back to my story… oh but you're here now and time is of the essence. We must be on our way," he said.

Anne gave a puzzled look and inquired, "An adventure, you say? I love an adventure, oh please may I come? I shall be ever so useful."

The rabbit sighed. "Oh well, I guess, but hurry up!"

And with that word, Liv tossed a ring to the floor and they all jumped in together.

4: A PINCH OF MAGIC

The new world was strange and interesting. Liv could see a dense forest, brightly coloured flowers and, looking through the canopy of trees, the most vivid rainbow she had ever seen. She heard the crunch of twigs and leaves underfoot.

A large, muddy hole had appeared below her and Liv fell in along with Anne and the white rabbit. The steep walls were slippery and as hard as she tried, she could not get out.

Through the loud blare of a growing wind in the trees, she heard a distant cackle of, "I'll get you, my pretty… and your little dog too!" and she heard a clank of rusty sounding metal grow closer as she saw a Tin Man staring down at her from above.

A lion and a scarecrow appeared around the hole with their leader, a girl with a pinafore dress and ruby red slippers.

They offered to help her and though Liv was tempted to take it, the old storm in her head would not let her accept. So, the group all trudged away disgruntled.

But as their voices died out, the cackle from earlier grew louder with violent yells.

Liv now knew who was coming: the Wicked Witch of the West. She turned towards the rabbit and Anne and shouted, "We have to get out!"

They all tried as hard as they could to pull themselves out of the hole but the witch's barbaric cry gradually edged closer.

Liv felt consumed by the darkness, trapped in her own thoughts. But she knew what to do as the witch bore down on her.

"Dorothy," she shouted and she clenched her fists together.

She opened her eyes by just a slither and realised a pair of sparkling ruby red slippers were being lowered into the hole and as she placed them on her feet, she saw the grinning Dorothy and all of her storybook friends.

Best of all, a tall glowing door was standing in the distance.

"You're welcome, Liv," said Dorothy, "and I hope you understand the lesson you've learned today."

After that big adventure, Liv was ready to go home, although she would miss her new friends. But that was all okay because Liv would try to make new friends back through the door and work in a team to accomplish things.

As she waved goodbye to Anne, the rabbit and Dorothy, she smiled to herself, grateful for their help.

Joyfully, Liv thrust open the illuminated door.

'There's no place like home,' she thought to herself.

DARK DIMENSIONS

Charles Hind

1

It was the dead of night after Dan finished his evening performance at school. The building was empty and he was the last one to leave. As the lights were turned off, he was filled with an ominous feeling. He thought he saw a shadow at first, staring at him in the left corner of the sports hall. Its eyes were glowing bright yellow and it seemed to have the proportions of a stick and was standing tall and intimidating. Dan turned the lights back on and it was gone. When the lights went off again, the figure was not there. Dan thought it was probably just his imagination.

He looked at the windows all closed up with the moonlight shining through. He could see the tiny specks of dust gliding through the air. Some of them seemed to glimmer in the spotlight. He was making his way to the fire exit door to leave the school when he realised the colour of the door was a dark blue when it was originally a dark green colour.

Now, just to clarify, Dan was not normally ever a scared or sensitive boy. He didn't believe in ghosts and he would have the bravery to explore an abandoned house without a coat or a torch, but this night, he was starting to wonder what the heck was going on! Slowly an urge came over him; he was going to open the door and if someone was there, he would definitely hurt them before they could hurt him.

When he opened the door, Dan felt a huge gust of wind smash against his face. Inside the door seemed to be a giant swirl of the colours pink, purple and red. But the most shocking thing that happened wasn't the portal, it was a black figure of a man with the proportions of a stick and bright, glowing yellow eyes! The same one he'd seen before! A voice seemed to come from the figure's head where the mouth would be.

"Please," the figure groaned.

"WHO ARE YOU!" Dan screamed in shock.

"Please put me back together," said the figure. "Will you help me collect my body from parts of this maze?"

Its voice was deep and intimidating. Dan was having flashbacks of every bad thing that happened in his life.

"WHO ARE YOU!" Dan screamed again.

"I am called Sven."

"WHY ARE YOU FORCING ME TO GO THROUGH AN ENDLESS MAZE THAT I AM MOST LIKELY GOING TO DIE IN?"

"I am not forcing you, I am asking you."

Suddenly, he looked less frightening and more vulnerable.

"W-wait, yes," Dan said hesitantly. "I will help you."

2

Dan leaped into the portal. Swirls of purple and pink were surrounding him, throwing him in different directions. And then… he opened his eyes. He couldn't see. It was total darkness. A faint voice surrounded him.

"Hello, Dan. You have chosen to go through a dangerous task," the shadow whispered. "You have been equipped with a flashlight, camera, food and water."

"Where are they?" Dan asked.

"On your right."

Dan picked up the items, checking them carefully.

"I can no longer speak or give you information," said the shadow ominously. "If I were you, I wouldn't ask why."

"Why?" Dan asked numbly, not thinking.

"SHUT UP!" screamed the shadow impatiently.

"Okay." The flashlight turned on. He saw that the place he was in was a maze with no lighting, yellow eroded walls and a stone floor.

Dan had a choice of three ways to go. There was also a huge stench in the air, something rotten. He started walking. The sound of his feet bounced around, the noise almost threatening. The maze was also wide and tall. The echoes seemed to get louder with every step he took.

He decided, for no reason, to go to the left side.

The maze was massive. He kept running into dead ends. Suddenly, Dan heard crying to his right. It sounded like a little girl.

"Hello?" Dan asked, his teeth chattering with fear, goosebumps rushing down his body all the way to his toes.

Around the corner, he saw a little girl in white, sitting in the corner, sobbing. He couldn't see her face but she had long, black, messy hair. He also couldn't see her hands because they were covered by the oversized white cloak she was wearing. In between her arms was a small, brown, dirty teddy bear. Dan slowly walked over to her and gave the girl a tap on the shoulder. She didn't move, but a ghostly finger pointed to the teddy.

The teddy bear seemed to be holding a letter. Dan picked it up. It said, "To whoever finds this letter, I just wanted to tell you that this is a dimension where you go through three of your biggest fears. I fell into this trap and have remained ever since. Your first challenge is a monster that can endanger your life. All the souls of his victims are trapped inside here. If you're reading this, I'm dead and if you continue so are you."

Dan put the letter down, his hand shaking even more.

Suddenly all Dan could see was swirls of pink and purple. He was now flying into another dimension. Dan felt his body slam into a chair. The ghost of the girl, teddy bear still clutched in her arms, appeared and warned him, "Don't take your eyes off them."

Dan frantically reached for his torch and flashed it around the room. Tall, black, elongated bodies surrounded him. He noticed as they inched forward, toward him, that he could never catch their actual movement. It was just that they were in one position, and when he looked again, they were in another. He also began to notice that they wouldn't step into the beams of his flashlight. Unfortunately, his flashlight could only throw off a small glow of light and the creatures were getting closer.

Panicking, he twisted his head from side to side looking for a way out and that is when he spotted the covered window. Dan got up. He dived to the side where the window was, barely missing an outstretched hand that would have ended everything.

Dan quickly spun round while grabbing the curtain at the same time. He screamed as the figure's face was three inches away from his. The eye sockets were hollow and it was grinning, showing all of its rotten, yellow, human-like teeth. A big waft of rotten breath hit him in the face, causing him to gag.

But the sunlight had done its job. The creatures began to crumble and collapse before his eyes.

"Congratulations, Dan," came the whisper of the shadow. "You have survived the first task and have restored part of the stick man. See how you do with the rest of the trial."

Pink and purple swirled around him and when it stopped, there was a faint buzzing noise of a VHS tape in the background. He was in a room where two large, open, metal safety doors stood on the left and four buttons were placed to his right. Two of them were coloured a dark dirty red with the words 'Door' underneath and beneath the door button were two more buttons coloured a bright white and which had printed underneath the words that read 'Lighting'.

Dan found himself looking at a screen, showing what seemed to be CCTV.

'I hate this,' Dan thought as a deep, rough voiced laugh echoed around him.

He looked to the stage on the screen and found three animatronics – a bear, a bunny and a bird. Suddenly, one flickered and then disappeared.

The bear was not there.

He quickly checked every single camera angle. One by one, the cameras glitched and went black and across his screen flashed the words, 'VISUAL ERROR'.

He pressed the lighting buttons, but nothing changed. He checked the digital clock and it read 3am! He knew this challenge. He had to last the night.

The cameras flashed back on and the maze was now a series of corridors.

When he checked the stage, all the animatronics had disappeared. Jumping through the cameras, he could see the bunny was in the dining area and the bird was in the right hallway. Where was the bear?

He checked the lights again.

The bird had moved and was now at the window on his right. Without hesitation, Dan closed the door, his heart almost leaping out of his chest with fear.

He checked the screen again.

There was another animatronic peeking out of the curtain of the stage, but this one looked different. It was thin, emaciated, the skin sagging. It looked like a zombie, holes and tears covering its body. The head was over long, while the mouth was filled with sharp teeth, discoloured and rotten.

Dan was reminded of the monsters from his previous challenge. Would the light help him this time?

The vision on the screen came into focus and Dan could make out that the latest animatronics was a fox. A very hungry fox.

Slowly it turned its head to the camera and once again the cameras flickered off, only for a short time before coming back up.

When it came back on, the fox had disappeared and the curtains were fully open. Dan frantically searched through the cameras to find the fox running toward the office he was sitting in. The echoes of footsteps pounded into every cell of his body.

More footsteps could be heard from the corridor to his left, these heavier, however, just as threatening. Leaping up, he flung himself at the door, leaning heavily against it to prevent anything from entering. The screen showed the other side of where he was, animatronics banging and battering to be let in.

Over the noise of screeching and banging, Dan heard the heavenly sound of chimes. It was 6am. Morning had come.

The noise from outside abated and nothing could be seen.

"You have survived the second trial. Nobody had got this far before. The stick man is gaining life. But you are not finished yet..." The hollow voice of the shadowy figure teased at his ears before Dan was once again swallowed by the swirls of purple and pink.

The first thing Dan noticed in the new room was the sound of giggling girls. The blackness of the room gave way and he could see groups and groups of girls, hair flicking and gossiping in loud whispers. Alone, in the middle of the room, being judged and ridiculed, Dan recognised this final fear. This was the biggest fear of all for him. The fear of being alone, of not fitting in. This was the one fear he thought he could not overcome.

The sound of the girls grew louder and louder, pressing in on his brain, clouding his ability to think.

It felt like the first day at school, when his loneliness had sent him home crying, his fear of never having a friend, never belonging.

How had he ever overcome that fear?

Crouched on the floor, head in his hands, Dan made himself as small as possible, hoping to disappear, to not be seen.

And then he remembered.

He remembered his friends from school. He remembered his family at home. He remembered the smiles from people he didn't know on his school bus. And he remembered that everyone was in the same situation.

Slowly Dan uncurled. He lifted his head and looked at the girls. They began to fade, to merge and become one person. One lonely person. And that person smiled.

It was the stickman. Only he wasn't a

stick, nor a man. It was a girl, around his own age, body intact and whole again.

"Thank you," she whispered as she too began to fade. "I can now rest, thank you."

Everything went dark.

Slowly, Dan saw the outlines of his eyelids opening.

Around him were a group of people he recognised. Teachers, students, friends, even potential friends. They were all looking at him with relief.

"You're back with us, Dan," said one of the teachers, kindly. "That was quite a knock on the head you got there. Can you stand up. Let's get you to the medical room to get you checked out."

Dan looked around him and saw he was back in the school. It was the middle of the day and everything was back to normal. He smiled. Everything was going to be okay.

CLEO OVERCOMES HER FEARS

Nicola Hatton

1

It was a Monday and Cleo already wished the week was over. She was standing at the entrance to her school in the foggy weather, shivering. Ancient and rusty, the gates stared down at Cleo, irritating her. A cracked and falling apart sign said: 'Thornberry School'. Cleo closed her eyes and hoped to be back at home. She didn't like school at all.

Suddenly, out of nowhere appeared a magical door. The door said, "Please answer the question and enter." Cleo was petrified and nervous to approach the door. The door had just spoken to her!

"What do you think is behind me?" said the door.

Cleo panicked. "I don't know." Wanting

it to be something she liked, Cleo blurted out, "Animals!"

The door answered, "Very well, that is your adventure."

Reluctantly, Cleo walked slowly towards the door, watching it open as she came closer. In the background she heard the head teacher shouting at wandering children, "Why are you not in your classroom?" A mumble of children's voices followed her as she stepped over the threshold of the door.

Cleo stopped and stared. Before her stood a small, brown monkey, with a friendly face and intelligent eyes. The monkey was wearing a bright yellow top with the logo 'Happy to Help'.

Cleo smiled in delight because she loved monkeys. However, she was also surprised and confused.

The monkey stepped forward and gripped her arm. "At last," the little monkey whispered, "somebody has come to help save us."

Cleo was alarmed at that. How could she help the monkey, if she couldn't even handle the bullies at school?

2

"My name is Polly," said the monkey as she pulled Cleo along with her.

Looking around, Cleo saw green trees surrounding her and through the trees she spotted a log structure. It was a hut, with open windows and a small wooden door.

Polly dragged Cleo toward the hut, furtively.

Inside the hut was a swarm of animals that were gathered, waiting in anticipation.

"What's this? What's going on?"

She was greeted with silence. She looked around at all the animals, waiting for someone to talk.

"Someone has come to rescue us," barked the dog.

"Rescue you from what?"

"It's the beavers, it's the beavers," all the animals shouted at once, causing Cleo to cover her ears in shock from the sudden noise.

Cleo pointed at the one beaver in the room. "Who, him?"

The beaver came forward and introduced himself. "I am Charlie. I have been making a plan to defeat the Beaver King and free my people from his cruel reign."

Polly stepped forward and explained, "This beaver is a good beaver and wants to help all the animals. The Beaver King is building dams and flooding the forest with water. All our homes are at risk."

"Let's go to the Beaver King's territory so we can show you his evil plans to redirect the rivers," said Polly.

3

They left the ruined hut and Charlie started leading the other animals through the winding trees. The dry dusty path began to change and Cleo's shoes started sticking in the mud.

The sucking noises followed them as they walked. They scurried across the damp dark ground, trying to avoid being stuck in patches of quicksand that had formed due to flooding.

The animals in the lead beckoned Cleo onwards. In their hurry to get through the forest, they missed their step and suddenly a large group of them fell into the earth.

Cleo gave a loud scream. She tumbled forward, rolling to the bottom of the hole in a rumpled heap. Slowly getting into a sitting position, Cleo groaned, "Ow, that hurt!"

Pulling herself together, she looked around to see who was with her. Charlie, a fox and a mouse had tumbled in with her.

All the other animals peered over the edge of the deep hole that they had fallen into. Concern and fear showed on their faces.

"Quick, run, the Beaver King's guards are coming," meowed the cat in an agitated tone.

The animals ran.

Looking up, Cleo saw a band of beavers in smart uniforms wearing the badge the Beaver King forced them to wear.

One of the beavers called to his party, "We have caught him! We have caught the traitor!"

The Beaver guards lowered a rope for the captured animals and Cleo to climb out of the hole. Once they had climbed out, they rushed the prisoners to the Beaver stronghold.

Shaking with fear, Cleo dragged herself along, terrified about what awaited her. This wasn't her world. She didn't know the rules. Was she going to die in a strange world, nobody knowing what happened to her?

Cleo and the animals were taken to the Beaver King.

"Take them to the cells," he said. "I will decide how to execute you later on."

Cleo sat in the cell, with her back to the wall, her arms around her knees and her head bent over. She was afraid. "Why am I here? I have done nothing wrong. All I did was come through a door and then the animals dragged me to that meeting!"

"Cleo. Are you alright, Cleo?"

She didn't answer.

"Don't worry, Cleo. I have a plan."

She looked up at Charlie, hope in her eyes.

"I managed to steal the key when the guards were throwing us into the cell," he explained. "As soon as dark comes, I will get us out of here."

A squeak came from Cleo's pocket and a furry head popped out, making Cleo jump in astonishment.

"I'm here," said the mouse. "I hid when the guards captured us. Do you want me to go and scout for you."

"Well done, they don't know you're here. Go and find out where the guards are."

4

When night time came, Cleo and Charlie left the cell, following the mouse quietly and passed the sleeping guards.

"Be quiet, I can hear a noise!" whispered Cleo.

"Someone is coming. Quick hide in here!" squeaked the mouse.

They could hear the sound of scurrying feet and voices talking low.

"Hang on, I can recognise the voice," said Charlie. "It's Polly the Parrott!"

Cleo dashed out of the hiding place excitedly and asked her what was going on.

"We're here to save you!" said Polly.

"You have fallen into my trap," said a deep voice.

They all turned around sharply, wondering what was going on.

In the entrance to the throne room, staring at them with a wicked evil grin, stood the Beaver King and his guards. His eyes were small and beady and glowed a strange yellow. He had long white whiskers and grey fur. On his head was an ornate crown with a sapphire blue stone gleaming in the candlelight.

"Now I am going to kill you all."

Charlie exclaimed determinedly, "Not without a fight you won't!"

A swarm of animals came together to fight the Beaver King and his guards. Cleo gave a gasp as the struggling animals pushed in front of her. She pushed past the fighting animals.

Cleo spotted Charlie and the Beaver King rolling on the floor in battle.

The Beaver King's crown flew off and Cleo caught it. The beaver king suddenly stiffened and all strength appeared to leave him.

Cleo shouted Charlie, "Charlie, I have got the crown. Take it so you are the new good beaver, make great choices and lead your people well."

When Charlie lifted the crown, the guards fell to their knees. "All hail King Charlie."

All the animals applauded and cheered King Charlie.

5

Cleo stood in the Beaver King's great hall the next day. King Charlie sat on his new throne and said to Cleo, "Thank you for all of your help. The land is saved and the forest is no longer flooded. Now we must get you home."

Cleo heard a noise. She glanced behind

her and saw a glimmering outline of a door shining in the sunlight.

"Oh no, it is the door," Cleo said to the animals. "I have to go now. Goodbye everybody and thank you. You made me overcome my fear of being shy. I am very determined to go back through the door as a stronger person. I hope I can come back someday to see if Charlie is doing a good job of ruling his land."

Cleo stepped through the door with a new confidence. She was standing at the entrance in the foggy weather, shivering. Ancient and rusty, the gates stared down at Cleo. She smiled. No longer afraid, she stepped into the new adventure of secondary school, declaring, "I won't be afraid anymore!"

THE INVASION

George Sapstead

1: COOKING ROOM

That day, the sun came up slowly. It was early December and it was an icy morning. There was frost all over the paths and windows. In the cookery room, Hope looked at Sophia and her friends helping each other clean up while she was waiting for her cake to bake. She was alone. She didn't want to help anyone.

When she opened the cupboard to start putting things away, she saw a mysterious tiny oak door with brass hinges. Wondering whether anyone would notice if she went missing, Hope pushed open the door and slipped quickly though the gap.

2: THE CASTLE

On the other side of the door, there were thousands of people wearing silver shining armour. Suddenly, the person in front of her stepped out of the way to reveal a steep drop. She was shocked at how high it was. As she walked backwards, Hope realised that if she took a few more steps, she would plummet into the icy cold water.

One of the men screamed at her to get her gear – her armour and bow.

Hope, who couldn't stand being told what to do, immediately felt a hot surge of anger. She pushed the guard back.

The guard lost his footing and slipped on a wet freezing cold puddle. He stepped up in a fit of rage and screamed at Hope, "Why did you do that?"

Hiding her face, Hope ran off into the castle, racing up the winding stairs, her heart beating fast like a drum. She stopped to look out from one of the watchers' windows and saw a sea of soldiers marching towards the castle.

3: THE DESTRUCTION PART 1

On the floor, Hope noticed a quiver of arrows next to a bow. She picked them up and ran up to the top of the castle stairs. Feeling threatened, she rained down arrows on to the soldiers below her. They began to pull out their shields, blocking the arrows that were firing towards them. They were now a sea of metal, and protected from her attack.

Suddenly, the archer she had pushed into the puddle appeared behind her, asking continuously, "Why did you push me over?"

She ran back down the winding stairs where she was surrounded by the men, who decided to take her to the dungeons to rot in the damp cells of the jail for hours.

'PLEASE, PLEASE LET ME OUT, I'll do anything you want!' Hope screamed at the top of her voice.

The guard told her that if she promised to fight to the death, she could come out.

She immediately went back up to defend the castle, firing arrows at the undefended soldiers.

4: THE DESTRUCTION PART 2

Unexpectedly, a man screamed, "Get off the walls!"

Hope ran down the stairs. Standing in the courtyard, Hope was preparing her bow, ready to fight the army who were trying to claim the land off the peaceful people who lived in the castle when suddenly the walls came crumbling down, creating a cloud of dust which covered the courtyard. She jumped out of the way and as the dust cleared, she was ready and aimed at the rival army's captain who was middle centre front row.

Releasing the arrow from her bow, it ricocheted around the walls, hitting the captain between the eyes. He groaned and fell to the floor with a THUD!

The opponent's army retreated to regroup and appoint another captain, continuing to challenge Hope and her troops.

Hope thought she had time to regroup… she was wrong.

5: THE FINAL BATTLE

Hope had barely caught her breath when the enemy (miraculously recovered) launched their next attack.

The enemy charged forward on horseback and cut off her escape back to the castle.

Hope found herself surrounded.

Boulders launched by catapults whistled through the air, hurtling towards the keep; they would surely break the castle defences and the battle would be over.

One of the catapults missed its target and hit a man who was in the crowd surrounding Hope. Looking around her, she saw a mass of people – priests and maids – ready to defend the castle in the final battle. Seizing the moment, Hope grabbed a sword dropped by the enemy and ran towards her gathering troops.

They looked at her, and she said, "We must work together to defeat this mighty army and win this battle once and for all."

As the troops ran towards the enemy, all working together, the unusual door appeared again and Hope thankfully went through it.

She was back in her cookery classroom and no one seemed to have noticed she was gone. Sniffing the air, she noticed that Sophia's cake was about to burn! Without thinking about it, she rushed off to help.

CONFLICT

Matheew Swift

1

Delilah was at school when the clock struck midnight. She ran through the school, panicked, petrified of what her parents would be thinking. She shouldn't be here. Her dad was the head teacher, and she had stolen his keys as a dare by her friends. A gloomy dark atmosphere surrounded her, and that added to her fear. Was her being here going to cause more trouble between her parents?

Delilah was stuck now and didn't know what to do. She had lost the key and couldn't find a way out. Her parents were going to go mad.

Suddenly, out of nowhere appeared a magical door. Was this a way out?

2

She walked through the door to find herself standing in front of her own house. The front door was different to the door that she was used to… it was the wrong colour. But at the same time, she recognised it. It was the door that had been there when her parents were together. Suddenly, her old primary school friend appeared next to her. Delilah jumped. Her friend was next to her because she was there to play with her. Delilah was puzzled.

3

Her friend Lily was dressed in their primary school uniform and she had the neon green glasses Delilah knew had been shattered the summer before. She saw a mirror of her own confusion on Lily's face.

"What's happening?" Delilah said.

"We're going to the park remember, silly," Lily said.

Suddenly, Delilah realised she was in the

past, from which she had been trying to escape for the last two years. A world filled with fear and chaos.

4

"Are you okay? You don't seem yourself today," Lily said.

Thinking Lily might tell her parents and make it worse, Delilah hesitated before saying, "Yeah, yeah. I'm fine. How about we just go to the park, for now?"

Lily replied, "That's what I've been talking about for the last week!"

So off they went to the park and on their way they met the people who were bulling them at school. This time instead of being frightened, Delilah stood up for herself and Lily and said, "You do this again, you will be in bother!"

The bullies said, "We are not afraid of you, Delilah."

"We'll see about that," said Delilah in frustration and without hesitation.

5

After Delilah and Lily left the park, they decided to go back home to see if anything had changed between Delilah's parents. She hoped that since she had stood up for herself and Lily that her parents would stop fighting. When Delilah went back home, she thought they would be arguing... but they weren't...

Instead, mum and dad were sat waiting for Delilah.

Mum said, "I'm sorry, I shouldn't have been such nuisance. I realised I had been starting the arguments... I feel like it is my fault".

Dad butted in, saying, "It wasn't your fault, not mine.... it was both of ours."

Mum and dad, both feeling upset, said they were tired of arguing and they were ready to apologise to Delilah for making her upset.

Delilah replied with an apology but she didn't know why she apologised. Except that she knew her parents were now back together and she could go back through the door to be in the future.

Now her parents were both at home. The house was all quiet. Teatime was mysterious and rather weird because both her parents were there and Delilah wasn't used to that.

Over the years, Delilah forgot that her parents had even divorced.

She even forgot about the door… or did she?

The door never appeared again. Delilah was sad. She never saw her friend Lily again because Delilah moved so far away. However, she was happy that she had two parents again, that were in the same home and loving towards each other and her.

THE BEAUTY OF BEING DIFFERENT

Rosie Turnbull

1: THE DOOR

It was Thursday evening, after school, and Mary Ann – a brave and different girl with grey eyes and bright red hair – was doing a school play. When the play had ended, she went to her house block to get her PE kit, feeling disappointed that yet again, none of her family had found the time to come and see her perform. The other cast members were walking away in a happy group – even the boy with the golden hair and emerald eyes who made everyone laugh and didn't know Mary existed.

Hearing thunder, Mary Ann grabbed her kit and ran. Outside, she couldn't see anything because of the icy fog that had descended. Suddenly, she saw a gleam of light in the corner of her eye. Terrified and freezing, she turned around and saw a small door only as high as her waist. Blinded by the fog, going through the door was her only choice.

When she got through the door, she blacked out.

When she woke up, her head felt a bit dizzy. She slowly got out of bed and looked at her alarm clock and saw the same date as the day before and realised she only had thirty minutes to get her clothes on, get her bag ready for school, eat breakfast, call on her friend and walk to school. She got ready and ran out of her bedroom. Mary took a step back as she saw a family photo in a frame. She stopped dead. Her dad was still tall but he had red hair not dark hair, her mum had red hair, not blonde the way it should be, and her brother had bright red hair. But something else was also different… their faces were the same as Mary Ann's.

Her mum shouted her and she ran downstairs. When she got downstairs, her brother looked the exact same as her and was watching her favourite chick flick movie. Her mum said that her breakfast was ready. Mary sat down at the table and asked where dad was. Her mum said he was at work early because he had to go to York that day.

Mary ate her breakfast and before long, her mum said, "Right come on, get your bag ready for school. Tonight is the big night!"

The play! But Mary was confused. Her mum never remembered about school plays. Never mind... Mary got her bag ready and headed out of the door.

2: COPY CAT

Mary walked to her friend's door and knocked. Her friend's mum answered the door.

"Oh, hi. Is Miley there?" Mary said.

"Do you mean Mary?" asked her mum.

"Umm I guess?" replied Mary.

Mary's friend, who in this strange

world through an even stranger door was apparently also called Mary, came to the front door and guess what? Bright red hair, and not only that, the same face.

"Hi, I will be out in a sec. Let me just get my bag," said Mary's friend.

"Okay," she replied, still very confused as to why suddenly everyone looked and sounded the same as her.

As they walked to school, they told each other about their weekend and surprisingly, they'd done the same things and gone to the same places. Mary remembered that it was an assembly morning. Usually, when she went to school, she expected everyone to look and stare at her – like they did every day. Her eyes downcast, she usually walked quickly to the sports hall without talking to anyone. But today, they didn't stare because they all looked just like her. Relief mixed with confusion ran throughout her body.

She quickly ran up the set of stairs and took a seat. Everyone waved to her and said hello.

Just before the head teacher was about to speak, the door to the sports hall opened. Everyone stared. It was a boy – a normal boy. That in itself made him strange, because everyone else was a 'Mary'. His hair was golden blond and his eyes sparkled emerald green. Mary knew who he was, she had stared at him from a distance for months. His name was Edward.

3

After assembly Mary went out for a break. Edward was sitting by himself. That was strange. Edward didn't ever sit by himself. Mary walked over and sat beside him.

"Hi," said Mary. "Your name is Edward, right?"

"Yes, and who are you?" asked Edward.

"Oh, sorry, I'm Mary from your school!" exclaimed Mary.

"Oh right…" said Edward, confused.

"You don't know who I am, do you?" queried Mary.

"Nope," said Edward, feeling embarrassed because he didn't know Mary.

Mary asked Edward how he got there. Edward explained the whole story and it was a repeat of her own story – a strange door in the fog. He'd barely finished the story when the bell rang.

"What class do you have next?" asked Edward.

"Geography," replied Mary.

"Oh, I guess we have the same classes," exclaimed Edward.

"We should probably get going or we will be late!" she suggested.

"Class," said the teacher as they went into the classroom, "we are going to finish the work we did last lesson, and when you are done, you can chat or draw."

All the kids got into their previous pairs and got to work.

Mary's friend called her over, patting the empty seat next to her and smiling.

Mary looked awkwardly at Edward. He didn't have a partner and no one was asking him to sit with them. He had to sit by himself.

When they finished their work, Mary said to her friend that she was going to talk to the new boy.

She sat next to Edward and they started to plan how to get back to the real world.

"Well, it is Thursday again, what if the same thing happens tonight?" Mary said.

"It might," said Edward.

"I have an idea! Okay, so tonight is the play, right?" said Mary.

"Yeah, I think," answered Edward.

"Okay, then, tonight when the play ends, how about we meet at the same place the door appeared?" suggested Mary.

Edward looked glad that there was a plan.

"Okay class," the teacher said, "make sure your desk is clean and head to your next lesson."

Their next class was PE so Mary and Edward couldn't work together because the boys and girls were separated for anything sports related. So, this lesson Edward was alone and had to find different friends. It wasn't usually hard for Edward to make friends, but here it was impossible. Everyone looked just like Mary and no one wanted to speak to him.

When it was time for lunch, everyone ran to the lunch hall. Edward watched as Mary went to sit with her Mary friends. No one wanted to sit with him so he sat by himself again.

He'd just finished his sandwich and was feeling a bit glum when someone sat next to him. It was Mary. His Mary. There was no mistaking the original Mary.

He smiled back as she smiled at him and started to talk more about their plan. When the bell went, everyone ran to their next class.

He didn't have any classes the same as Mary and he sat on his own in each one, no one talking to him, but plenty of people staring. It wasn't nice.

At the end of the school day, he ran to the theatre and was relieved to see Mary there already. They got their costumes on and the play began. Luckily, everyone had the same roles as before. The play went well. Edward was pleased to see Mary so happy and waving to her family in the audience. His mum wasn't there. His mum didn't ever miss any of his performances. The day was just getting worse.

When the play ended, they headed out to the exact spot where the door had been but... no door.

Edward looked around, dismayed.

He had to get back to his reality.

4

The next day at school, Mary looked for Edward but he was nowhere to be seen. She was frantic. Where could he be?

She snuck out at break and went back to the spot where the door had appeared in the fog, and there he was.

"Why aren't you in lessons?" Mary asked.

Edward admitted in an embarrassed voice that he hated it and that he hated everyone because the other Marys were mean to him.

Mary felt sad about this and decided to set herself a task to change Edward's mind.

She offered him a compromise... she suggested that if he went back to school with her, she would talk to him and she would let everyone else know that he was nice even if he did look different.

Edward agreed and they went back to school.

The day went very quickly and one by one people started to stare a bit less and talk to Edward a bit more. Before they knew it, it was after-school club time.

It was a drama club, so Mary and Edward went to the club together.

"Are we still going to look for the door at the end of this club?" Edward asked.

"Absolutely," Mary said. "I want to go home too! Even though this place is kind of nice."

When the club ended, Mary and Edward went to the place where the door had appeared.

Just as they hoped, it stood exactly where it had when they come through it at the start of their adventure.

5

When they crawled through the door, they both ended up at their own houses. When Mary snuck into her house, both of her parents rushed to her.

"Where have you been?" asked her mum.

"We have been so worried!" added her dad.

"At Miley's house for a sleepover!" Mary said, very nervously, hoping they would believe her.

"Well, why didn't you text us?" asked her dad.

"My phone was out of charge and they didn't have one that would fit my phone's charging port," answered Mary.

"Anyway, the important thing is that you're home and that you're okay," her mum said, relieved. "Isn't tonight the night of your play at school? We'd love to come."

That day at school, Mary saw Edward. They looked at each other and smiled.

In that moment, Mary realised that it is good to be different and any time she felt bad about herself, she could look back to this day.

She realised it is good to be different, and she didn't need to be ashamed of who she was. Secondary school was just another opportunity to make new friends and meet new people.

Huntcliff School, Saltburn

IMAGINARY

Sophie Allan

Autumn and Amelie walked through a door in school and were scared about their maths exam. So, they were running around the school and they saw a mysterious door. It took them to the magical woods. The trees were damp and green and it was dark. They were scared. Autumn and Amelie walked through the woods in exactly twenty-four hours.

After one hour, they found massive footprints in the mud. They followed the huge footprints that led to a big furry, friendly monster.

The big blue furry monster was called Cuddles and gave a hug to everybody. Cuddles held a paw out for them to shake. They held each other's hand and walked through the dark mysterious woods.

They saw animals such as squirrels, birds

and mice. After they had seen the animals, they came across a fallen tree. They thought their way was blocked but then Cuddles had an idea. She helped Amelie and Autumn over the fallen tree by picking them up with her big, strong arms.

Suddenly, a big wolf came in front of them and was being nasty to them. He was howling at them and they were scared. The wolf was grey with some fluffy bits around his neck and his teeth and claws were as sharp as a thorn.

Cuddles shouted at the wolf, "Go away!"

Cuddles moved her arms which frightened the wolf because he was scared of shadows and Cuddles had a really big shadow. So the wolf ran away back to his home. They walked the way Cuddles thought was the way to the shortcut to the magical door.

Once they found it, they walked through the bright door back to their school and told everybody the story. They told their mam that they heard a wolf howl and her mam said that there were no wolves near here, it was just their imagination. When everyone knew about the story, they all laughed and they said it wasn't true but it was, so they argued for a while till they all agreed it was true. Cuddles was still by their side and she was helping them with their homework and was in their exam. They were not scared of wolves anymore. Whenever they are scared now, they imagine Cuddles with them and are not frightened.

THE MYSTERY ELEVATOR

Isaac Basham

Lorenzo looked at the map on the wall at school and saw the sign for the elevator. He walked there and he went in and pressed the button. The elevator shot down as fast as lightning and kept going down for a long time. Lorenzo thought, 'What is going on and what is happening?'

It suddenly hit the floor and he walked out into a dark, mysterious cave. As he turned around, the elevator vanished.

Lorenzo felt scared and worried because he could not see anything. He needed a light. He searched around and felt a box and felt there was wood inside. He rubbed sticks together for a long amount of time until he had a fire. He felt better because now he could see as he was scared of the dark.

He went further into the cave and used

a stick with a fire on to see where he was going and saw a light coming through the bottom and the top of a door, as if it was glittering.

Lorenzo thought, 'I can use the light coming through the door and it will be better than the fire.' He was in the doorway for five minutes and suddenly he was hit by lightning. He started to see things in front of him, a lot of dark things and his fear was the dark. His vision went black and he hit the ground.

He could feel something on his body and woke up. There was darkness all around him and he heard the noise of the elevator door, then he remembered where he was. Still in the cave. He was having flashbacks. The cave was all light around him. But the light was coming from his eyes. He could see in the dark!

He used the light coming from his eyes to go deeper into the cave and saw the door again but this time it was a different colour and he knew if he went in it, something good or bad could happen. He decided to go further in and there was a dark corridor. The light in his eyes suddenly went out. Then he went down the corridor and then when he exited the corridor, the light in his eyes came back and he saw cobwebs and then he heard a noise and when he looked up, he saw a huge spider.

Lorenzo felt a surge of power as the spider was coming down. He saw it as a villain and so he had the mindset to defeat it. As it was coming down, he tried to break the cobwebs so it couldn't come down anymore.

It tried to climb the walls and fell to where he was. They started to attack each other and then someone appeared next to Lorenzo and the random person shouted, "No, don't hurt the spider."

The person who had come through the door had superpowers too. They could talk to animals and explained why they shouldn't hurt the spider. It was lost and needed to get home. They could also make lightning appear from their hands to help the spider. They moved their hands in round rotations to create lightning. Then they were out of energy so they couldn't use their powers. Lorenzo realised he had to help even though he was scared and worried and thought he couldn't do it on his own.

He tried to help the mysterious person by asking if he could transfer power to them. The mysterious person didn't reply for a long amount of time so when he looked at the spider, it reached the ground. Lorenzo and the mysterious person used their powers to help the spider. Lorenzo used his powers to see in the dark and the mysterious person used their powers to create lightning and create a portal, which sent the spider home.

He was so happy, so was the mysterious person who was a girl. He found out her name was Alysa and they were now best friends and she was the same as Lorenzo but she defeated a huge spider on her own and she had got there the same way Lorenzo did, through an elevator. She had been there longer than Lorenzo had and had way more experience than Lorenzo.

Lorenzo felt jealous but he decided to find a way out of this.

He thought he had to before another massive thing came and they had to defeat that and go through what they did before and Lorenzo wondered why his super strength didn't work in that cave.

Alysa knew something was off and she couldn't word it and it was on her mind all day but Lorenzo said to Alysa, "If we find an elevator, we both can get out."

He didn't need to be jealous of Alysa… he needed to work with her.

She said, "Where are we going to find an elevator out in the middle of nowhere?"

Lorenzo said, "Well, if we find a building we can."

"A building where?" said Alysa. "If we get lucky, we might find one, I don't know where but it's possible."

"Probably we might find an abandoned place. I don't know… well, it's a worth looking, isn't it?" said Lorenzo.

"Well okay," said Alysa so they went and walked and walked until they saw something in the distance; it was massive.

"I think it's a building," he said so they walked up to it.

"Wow," said Alysa.

It was a massive hotel and it was so big it had to have an elevator so they went and looked around and they thought it was haunted because there were random doors shutting and things falling off the shelves and then Lorenzo shouted, "There it is… the elevator!"

Lorenzo and Alysa walked through the door and when the elevator stopped, they walked through into the school corridor.

Much later, Lorenzo found a spider and kept it as a pet. And whenever Lorenzo is scared now, he remembers his adventure with the spider and is not afraid of the dark anymore.

GHOST STORY

Brooklyn Coonan

John was walking through the school hallway and found a mysterious glowing door. He walked through the door and found himself in a dark, spooky cemetery. He started to look around and found that there were some people there also. But it turned out that they were not people. They were ghosts. He started to back up in fear. The ghosts turned around and he ran as fast as he could but the ghosts were catching up… until he fell into a giant hole.

He fell into a massive underground cave, so he started walking through the cave and he found a giant spider on the wall that started charging at him, so he ran and he eventually found an exit.

He ended up in front of an abandoned house. When he entered the house and he went upstairs, he saw the same giant spider from the cave. He ran out of the room, down the stairs into a different room, opened a crate and got a machete. He ran back upstairs to fight the spider but when he went back upstairs into the room, the spider was gone and the window was smashed with glass all over the floor.

He wanted to find the spider so he started running around. Eventually, he found a giant cave so he went in and there were lots of little spiders on the walls so he had to be very quiet.

When he saw the giant spider, he noticed it was see-through, which told him that it was a ghost spider. It used one of its long legs to write out that it was lost on the cave floor. John decided to help it. The spider wrote on the cave floor the words: 'Find other ghost spiders'.

John and the spider started to explore the other caves, then John heard a banging noise. As they got closer, they saw it was the other ghost spiders. They looked happy to see him. The big spider used its leg to spell out 'Thank you' on the cave floor.

"You're welcome," replied John.

The spider drew the shape of a door on the cave floor and the door appeared. John went through and found himself back at school. He is not scared of ghosts or spiders anymore.

THE CLOWN CHASE

Amaya Cooper

As Alina walked through school, the lights suddenly went off. She went to her friend and her friend said, "What is happening?"

Alina whispered, "Shhh, they have turned the power off."

"Why?" her friend asked, frightened.

"We are late out of school, but it's fine, now hurry before Miss Crow sees us."

The girls were scared of Miss Crow because she looked like a horrible old crow and she was very strict.

As the girls walked through the school, they saw a glowing door. As they moved closer to the door, they saw a hand reaching out and grabbing them and…

When Alina woke up, she woke her friend Yasmin up and whispered, "Yasmin, wake up."

"Why? Leave me alone, mum."

"Ha ha ha, I'm not your mum. It's me, Alina."

"Oh hi, Alina. What's up?"

"Open your eyes."

Yasmin blinked. "Where are we?"

"I... um don't know. I think we're in a tent. Let's look outside." It was dark and all they could see were trees moving. They got their torch and got out of their tent and looked around.

It was so dark, they fell in a well. They slipped and they ended up somewhere where there was light. They shouted for help and a young man came and said, "Here's some ropes. I'll tie them on now."

They climbed up and thanked the young man, whose name was Oakenly.

As they walked away, he said, "Wait. Do you need anywhere to stay?"

They said, "Yes."

Oakenly said, "I know a hotel. I'll take you there."

As Oakenly paid, he said, "I'll meet you at the lobby tomorrow for a grand tour around New York."

Yasmin and Alina both said, "Ooooh, sounds great."

But as they walked into the hotel room, they saw a door glowing. As they crept closer to the mysterious door, they touched the handle and as they touched the handle, it opened by itself.

As it creaked open, they saw a brown chest with gold hinges.

Was it treasure?

They started to head towards it but as they reached for it, they saw a clown. The clown had a bat with blood on it and it swung the bat at the girls.

They both shouted, "Ahhhh!"

They ducked and ran but didn't get out.

They picked up a bucket of water and chucked it and ran… straight into a portal and ended up in the woods. They walked through the woods until they saw an underground bunker.

There was a huggable monster that always wanted hugs off of people and when they saw it, they ran back into the woods to a tent.

They knocked on the tent and went in where they saw an old couple who looked and smelt like they had NEVER shaved, or showered.

"Hello," said Alina and Yasmin.

"Hello," said the old couple. "Who are you?"

"We are Alina and Yasmin. What's your name?"

"Our names are Miss and Mr Rough. What are you girls doing in the woods so late?"

"We just got chased by a clown!" said Yasmin.

"A CLOWN?" said Miss Rough.

Mr Rough laughed. "A clown, you silly. Who would be scared of a clown?"

Just then, they heard something rumbling in the bushes outside. They saw a flash of lightning and a sword appeared.

Alina picked it up and held it out in front of her.

A figure stepped out of the bushes.
IT WAS THE CLOWN.

The clown stood as still as a statue.

It smiled at them and they realised it looked like Miss Crow.

Still gripping the sword, Alina turned and ran. The clown followed. Alina turned and raised the sword.

"Good," the clown said, "you now have the power to confront your fears."

And with that the clown disappeared.

A big purple portal appeared, they jumped in and were back at school. They weren't scared of Miss Crow anymore. When they're scared now, they always remember the sword. Alina and Yasmin are old now and still remember their adventure.

THE MYSTERIOUS DOOR

Ruby Donaghy

As Frankie was sitting in the school office, she was filled with worry because she was scared that someone would bully her because she had just been diagnosed with ADHD a few weeks ago and some people said that was a disability.

As she sat there, she noticed a pink door and came closer to it. She pushed through the door and entered a long, narrow corridor. As she walked further in, it got more narrow and she eventually found a key with her name on. Realising it must be for her, she picked it up and searched for another door.

After hours of looking, she finally arrived at the door. It was another small pink door but this time it had a shiny gold handle. She started to open the door… and it tripled in size. It was double her height!

As she walked through, she heard rustling in a bush and walked over to it. She looked inside and saw a dog called Ralph. He said he was a sidekick for a girl called Frankie. However, he'd not been able to find her for four years.

Frankie said, "I'm Frankie. Why do you ask?"

Ralph said, "I need help on a secret mission to find all the animals and people in planet Zorg."

As they went to find them, Ralph talked. "I have some friends I want you to meet, they will help us along the way."

"Okay," Frankie said.

As they arrived at Branston Bunny's house, they stepped into his underground rabbit hole where their space rocket was. They jumped inside with everything they needed and went to planet Marsbar where they needed to save all the animals from the crocodile Jack that had been stealing all the animals to eat them.

They all decided to make a plan to defeat Jack by capturing him and taking him to planet Zorg. So, they created a cage out of sticks. The crocodile came. Everyone was scared of it.

But although he was camouflaged, Frankie's ADHD allowed her to see him. As she looked at him, she noticed he was different, like her, and did not look like a fierce crocodile at all.

As they lured him in, the crocodile climbed into the cage and they shipped him to Manchester Zoo – with all the other crocodiles! Where he was very happy and got fed three times a day.

With a BANG! Frankie was back at Huntcliff School in the waiting room, ready to go into school, with no fear at all. She didn't care what other people think of her ADHD and what they thought of her. She'd showed her bravery and realised that ADHD wasn't a disability at all, it was a super power.

THE CITY OF CLUES

Alexxa Hutchinson

"Quick, hurry," said Delilah.

"Where are we going?" asked Asayna.

The corridor was as quiet as the moonlight except for the scuffling of three people's feet.

"GIRLS! STOP WHERE YOU ARE, YOUNG LADIES!" screamed Mrs Gatherdstone.

They had run out of a lesson to prepare for the Maths exam next period. As Miss said that, Angel's heart was pounding, as she tensed all her body up and looked like she was going to cry. This is because she was shy.

"What are we going to do?" Angel said with a hint of fear in her voice.

"Quick, get in here!" Delilah pulled open the door and threw her friends through and pulled the door closed with a crash to reveal not a classroom but a busy city bustling with people. The noise was as loud as a football crowd, roaring like they were in the World Cup.

Angel grabbed the person next to her and had a breath of panic before she nearly passed out in a faint.

"Where are we?" Asayna said in a whisper with a squeaky voice as if she had a cold.

"No idea at all," said the others girls in unison.

Delilah (being the clever one in the situation) said, "Maybe we should get off the main road before we get run over."

"Great idea," said Angel in a mousy voice, and, as quick as a flash, they got off the road immediately.

"Now what? Where are we? How do we get back before the exam?" Asayna said in a scared voice.

"WOW it's stunning," Delilah exclaimed in awe as she saw the famous New York billboards in front of her amazed eyes. "Can you see? We are in the famous New York."

As they wandered through the city, they entered a grand hotel with golden outlines all over the white walls. An old woman came scuttling towards them with a hood over her head and passed an old, wrinkly letter with no address on it and she ran off without a word.

As they opened the letter, a hot breeze surrounded them.

The note looked old and torn and had a stain on it across the page in fancy writing that said:

As I thought, you are reading this. You went through a door and found yourself in a completely different place. You're not the only ones that this has happened to. You have to go round different places to find clues and find the right thing to get through to home and be careful.

The woman who gave them the letter suggested they look in the hotel library.

When they got there, they found a section about maps and saw that there was an unknown map at the top of the shelf. They found some steps and looked at the map. The map was of New York and had lots of roads and secret paths still unknown.

"We need to go and look around quick if we want to get back before the test and before Mrs Gatherdstone finds out we are missing or until they call our parents and tell them we are missing from school and then they will call the police, then we will be put in jail, then see our life is ruined forever, then we can't see anyone forever, then we will die alone and it will be all our fault," explained Angel with a tear in her eye, like she was going to cry.

"Don't worry, it's going to be okay," Delilah said. "We will find our way out and it will all be fine. Anyway, Miss will enjoy the peace and quiet while she has it, won't she? So don't worry at all. We will be completely fine and we won't get caught by the police or die, okay? We need to find the clue. So where do you suppose we start then?"

"Well, as you have asked, we should go to one of the best places in New York and our home town."

"Bobba?" asked Angel in a confused voice.

"Exactly. We love going there, don't we, so it could be there."

As they went outside, the billboard flashed with 'Are you thirsty? Do you need a drink? Well come in! Bobba Moler in the centre of every major city and town.'

"Off we go now before it closes and soon it will be pitch black and we can only see by the light."

As they entered the shop, the breeze of Bobba came over them.

They looked around and they saw a note on the wall but it was at the highest point on the wall and the only way to get to it was to go on each other's shoulders and catch it so that is what they did exactly and they got the paper but they all collapsed down into a pile and GOT THE NOTES!

Suddenly, they thought they had the last clue but of course they didn't. It was late and they were tired and the clue was that they needed to find something unusual that things were posted into. Of course this was the easiest clue ever. It was a post box but this was not the easiest clue to find because, can you guess, there are 7,000 post boxes in New York and with it being late, it could take a while.

They all sighed as they slumped back on the wall.

"What are we doing to do?" said Angel. "It is so late, I am so tired, cold, hungry and worried."

"Well, there is only one thing to do," said Delilah. "We've got to get to all 7,000 post boxes by sunset so off we go!"

Post box after post box after post box. It was 2am.

"I'm too tired to go on," Delilah said.

It was most unlike Delilah to give up.

Asayna didn't know what to do but she didn't want to let her friends down, and she didn't want them to give up.

She stood up and looked around… only a short distance away was an unusual post box… it was green!

"This has to be it!" she shouted.

As they went close and were about to touch a post box, for what felt like the 100th time, they inhaled a whiff of lavender-smelling air and found themselves back at school, safe and ready.

Before this Angel was very shy and

unconfident and now she is confident and less shy because of facing her fear in a big city with loads of people. Whenever she is frightened now, she thinks about what she did in the city and isn't frightened anymore. They all became best friends forever after that.

THE BOY

Jayden Leader

Joseph was walking to school, twiddling his fingers, worrying as usual, that everyone was always laughing at him. This frightened him because he was terrified of being laughed at.

Just then he saw a magical door. When he saw the door, he was curious so he went through it and then he passed out. He woke up in a mysterious place.

There was pink grass, green trees and purple sky. He was confused. There were lots of weird shaped animals. Then he could hear lots of loud footsteps and loud thumps and then there came a giant beast. The beast was really hairy with massive ears and short legs. It had the head of a pig and the body of a dinosaur.

It made a noise like the rumble of an earthquake. Joseph was terrified that he was about to be stamped on but then the beast just walked straight past him. It was friendly.

It bent down and smiled at Joseph and then carried on walking. Joseph was shocked – he wasn't used to anyone smiling at him, let alone a beast.

Joseph was curious so he followed it. It went to a giant rock that had a secret door. When he went through the door, the giant dinosaur who smiled at him wasn't actually a dinosaur. It was a man in a costume.

But the man did not know there was someone behind him. The man screamed. He was shocked.

They both screamed.

"It's just me," said Joseph, smiling.

But the man said, "Shush… the real beast, it's outside. The beast has small ears, a big hairy head and is very mean."

They went to the secret door and watched as the beast hunted its prey. But the more, Joseph watched, the more he realised and started to understand that the beast wasn't mean and chasing people… it was injured. It was trying to get help.

Later that night, Joseph and the man were geared up, ready to help the beast. They went looking but they could not find it.

Thirty one days later, they were starting to run out of food. They had to find the beast. Suddenly, the beast was running after them. They were frightened, but luckily, they were geared up. The beast grabbed onto Joseph and, using the first aid kit he had, he helped to heal the beast's injured hip. The beast wasn't afraid anymore.

The magical door appeared. Joseph went through the door and was back in school. He wasn't afraid of people laughing at him anymore and was very confident about what he did in life. He'd realised that sometimes someone who looks angry and scary is just hurt and might need a friend.

Now Joseph has lots of friends.

THE REALITY

Eva-Rose Maynard

Phoebe was a bright girl, shy, pretty with long blonde hair and blue eyes. In secondary school she was bullied for being too pretty as people were jealous of her.

She was on the way to her locker and saw the girl that was picking on her. The nearest room was the PE changing room but instead of the usual door, there was a bright flash of light. She looked behind her and realised she was by her locker and the girl who was picking on her was coming towards her and she panicked.

Lucy was taller than Phoebe and was known for causing fights. "Hi Phoebe, how are you? I haven't seen you for a couple of days."

Phoebe was confused at this act of kindness and she replied with a hesitant, "Hi."

As she was on her way to Maths, everyone

was giving her compliments about how nice she looked today and how her clothes were very nice.

This made her feel weird because no one had ever talked like this before to her. She thought this was all very strange.

Phoebe saw her friend Sophia and asked her, "What's going on?"

"Wow," Sophia said, "are you actually talking to me? I never thought one of the popular girls would actually talk to me!" And off she went, very excited.

Later Phoebe saw her music teacher walking down the hall towards her and she thought she was going to ask her about how the new song was going. Instead, the teacher just walked past.

"Miss Right!" Phoebe called. "Have you got my writing book for my song in your office because I thought I gave it to you but I can't find it at home."

"Hello," Miss Right said, "I'm confused. Who are you?"

Phoebe started laughing, thinking it was a joke. "Have you seen it?"

Miss Right walked away, ignoring Phoebe. That was not normal.

Phoebe started to think about her music and started rhyming in her head. She did this to keep herself calm.

She was still her normal self but in a fake world and no one knew about her music.

She went to her locker then opened it to get her chemistry book out then she saw a flash of light. Suddenly she was back in the real world like nothing ever happened.

She realised the fake world wasn't how she thought it would be and accepted herself for who she was. She made a friend group who accepted her and liked her, and more importantly, liked her music. Phoebe was more happy and joyful and less caring about what people thought of her. Maybe secondary school could be great, after all.

HERO

Kadee-Lee Philips

She had her breakfast as she was walking to school. She walked to form and said hi to her mate as she did so, then she went to her math class. She wrote the date in her book but the teacher was going to the printer in the maths office and she decided to check the time on her phone. But just as she did, he walked back into the room and told her to please get off her phone and put it on his desk.

He asked her to go to the maths office so that they could have a chat. She waited for about two minutes and she got bored waiting. She looked around the room and saw this weird, brown, old, modern door and she also saw a key lying next to it. She thought that maybe that key was for the door. So she decided to grab the key and try it out. As she did, she was dragged in by a weird current and there it was… the stable was waiting for her.

As she started to walk through, she saw the memories of her horse Hero flipping onto her, breaking her rib only because he had never done a team chase before. He was scared and so was she. She knew that this was the end but she was lucky as the only two bones she had broken were one rib and her left arm. But it was her dominant arm so now she didn't know what to do. She was lost in confusion and she was terrified to go back to the barn where Hero was but her Mum was encouraging her to go back. As a wise old woman told her Mum, even if you fall, you must get back on!

As she listened to those words, she thought about it for a couple of seconds before saying yes. Her Mum told her, "Get your helmet, get your protection jacket and get your boots. Your tack should still be at the stables. Get ready to get in the car. We're about to set off after I've had my coffee."

While she waited, she was looking at

photos of her and him, looking at the team chase, and she came upon the one of her falling off. Seeing that, she lost a bit of confidence. As butterflies grew bigger in her stomach, she tried to gain back the confidence as she looked at the positive ones. Her Mum called her over and said, "Get the car keys, I'm almost done."

She ran to the door, grabbing the keys, and jumped into the car.

An hour later, she had arrived at the stables. You could hear his jolly neighs coming from his stall. She already lost more confidence as she arrived. As she saw him, she lost more confidence, thinking of the fall. She quietly asked her Mum to groom him and to tack him up for her.

As he was ready to go, her Mum said, "Wait, let me tack up my horse real quick."

She waited with Hero, getting some treats from the feed room. She called to her Mum saying, "Are you finished?"

Her Mum said, "Yes, let me get Butterfly a treat."

She mounted Hero. Her Mum got on her own horse and said, "Why don't we take the meadows?"

She agreed. They both started cantering through the meadows when her Mum said, "There's a jump. It's perfect for you and Hero."

As her Mum leaned forwards, approaching the jump, she leaned forward. Butterfly jumped first.

Hero followed on. She lost her reigns while she did. She panicked, holding onto his mane but as she landed perfectly with Hero, she felt like she was already in the cross-country course. She was so happy. She gave him a treat for his good behaviour.

Her Mum was full of joy. She even said that she had already paid for her cross-country course next week. She was shocked as she hadn't asked for it. But at the same time, she was glad. Her and her Mum continued doing the jumps ahead.

Hero galloped back to the stable with her Mum. She jumped off and her Mum untacked Hero and Butterfly. She was over the moon.

In the stables, she saw a door. The door took her back to school. She walked in and the teacher greeted her. At the beginning, she had been on her phone to text her Mum that she felt sick but she had just been nervous. Now she is more confident and does not feel sick anymore. And she is looking forward to that team chase with Hero…

THE MAGICAL DOOR

Esmerelda R

Betty didn't have any friends at school because she was a loner, because she was so pretty and other people were jealous of her. This made her feel cool because she thought she was better than them. Or at least she thought she was.

Betty went through the door on the school corridor and fell and landed on an escalator which took her to Primark. She walked in and the lights started flickering. Then she went round to the tills and there stood Bigfoot. The beast gave her a nudge and shot her into a different tropical land.

She was scared as she looked around. She saw a cave ahead so she wandered towards it.

She panicked as she went in, but she took a deep breath and stepped forward, then in the distance she spotted a beautiful horse.

She decided to name the horse Layla. Layla was a bit anxious when they first met but eventually they became friends. Betty asked if she could hop on.

Layla neighed so they went off and they were cantering quite happily but then they fell down a hole and landed in a really big freezing place.

At the top of a mountain stood a Bigfoot family.

This was the Bigfoot that had pushed her into this other land.

Betty looked at the Bigfoot creatures.

They were quite ugly.

But the baby Bigfoot was super cute.

"Come with me," she shouted and the baby Bigfoot jumped onto Layla and off they rode.

All of a sudden, they slipped.

They fell down an ice slide into freezing water that was cold enough to turn you as numb as a plumb.

They kept sinking and finally got to the

bottom of the icy cold sea. They all flipped upside down and it felt like the sea dropped them into a creepy place.

In this really mysterious place, there was a massive witch. When I say massive, I mean big big, which well, she looked like a witch. She was a horrible ugly figure with long spiky claws. The witch wore a big black gown with a long green spotty hat.

The baby Bigfoot was scared.

Even though they were under water, they could speak.

"Don't hurt us," cried Betty.

"Why would I hurt you?" said the witch.

"Because you're an ugly old witch," Betty said.

"Witch I am," she said, "but ugly…? Why would that make me want to hurt you? You are very pretty, Betty. And you, little baby Bigfoot, are very cute, but you are still a monster. And you, Layla… you are a beautiful horse, but does that make you perfect?"

Layla neighed.

And the baby Bigfoot roared. Because he was in fact a monster and he knew it.

Betty looked at the witch and the horse and the baby Bigfoot.

"I can help you," said the witch, "but only if you look inside yourself and see that beauty is only skin-deep... Look at others as they really are, and you may find yourself some real friends."

Betty realised that she wasn't better than anyone, and she realised that she quite liked having friends.

The witch snapped her fingers with a smile.

And Betty ended up back in Primark where she started. She went back down the escalator and fell backwards upside down through the door! Back where Betty had started at school but as she looked around her, she saw people as they really were. Kind and happy and helpful, and that's what she wanted to be too.

Laurence Jackson School, Guisborough

THE PUZZLE

Jeff Bails

It was a warm spring day in the school playground. The white fluffy clouds floated past whilst the birds were singing. In the rays of sun, children were screaming with happiness. Everyone except Robby. He was alone.

Robby looked up and noticed a door he hadn't noticed before. He went through it, but no one even noticed he had gone.

It took him to a dark room. There was a boy sitting on his own, crying in the corner and he said "hello", but it seemed he was like Robby, who had no friends.

Robby tried the door that had brought him there, but it was locked.

The boy had ginger hair and green eyes and old clothes. Next to the boy was a puzzle – a jigsaw – with 3001 pieces. There was a timer next to it and a sign overhead telling them that they had to beat the record that was 12 minutes and 5 seconds.

Robby said he would try to do it on his own – for seven months since the fight with his friends, he had got used to being alone and having no help.

As he placed the pieces together, he saw his own face appear but unusually, he was smiling. Placing the next piece, he saw a strand of ginger hair and realised it was the boy he had just met.

Looking up at the clock, he saw ten seconds left – he would not make it. A sound like a siren went off, leaving Robby feeling extremely frustrated.

Robby looked at the boy next to him and asked him, "What's your name?"

"Seb," he replied, his voice timid but friendly.

The siren suddenly sounded again, and the boys looked up at the timer – it now read: "You have only one chance remaining."

They knew the only way out was to work together.

Seb suggested that he focus on the sky and the background and Robbie focus on the people. They knew that as soon as they touched the pieces, the timer would start.

Hands ready, they glanced at each other quickly and smiled. They began.

They completed it in 12 minutes and 4 seconds. A green light glowed along with a sound like a till opening.

The door opened.

As they walked back into the warm spring day, they saw a smile reflected in each other's faces. In the sunshine, they started to play, and joined in with the laughter of the other children.

THE SCHOOL LOCKDOWN

Jaiden Bousfield

Jaiden and Oliver had just been to their locker. When the lockdown alarm went off, they were on their way to a maths class – late. They would probably be in trouble. Everyone always thought the worst of them.

The Headmaster said over the speaker, "Go into lockdown."

Everyone except Oliver, Jaiden and a child called Harry went to the room.

Harry was nice and very well behaved.

Jaiden said, "I cannot believe that they have put the school in lockdown."

Meanwhile, Harry shouted loudly, "Guys, are there zombies outside?"

Oliver replied, "Hey, they're not zombies. You are too paranoid."

It might not have been zombies, but there was clearly something going on outside –

so Jaiden, Oliver and Harry proceeded to try and find out what was going on.

Suddenly a loud and abrupt noise filled the air.

"What was that?" uttered Oliver.

Harry, Jaiden and Oliver carried on walking towards the noise, intrigued to see what it was but intimidated by the possibility of what it might have come from. They went through the lunch hall up the stairs to S12 (a science lab). Surprisingly, they heard what sounded like shelves being tipped and thrown about.

Suddenly, the door swung, swiftly open and this was followed by a blood-curdling scream.

"We should go," Jaiden said shakily.

They went straight to the door - not realising it looked different. Through the door were dense trees.

"It's not sunset yet," Harry said.

Oliver interrupted, "In case you didn't notice, Harry, we're in a forest!"

The group carried on walking and noticed a sound coming from above. They ignored it for a while. Walking through the forest, they fell into a mysterious, mirrored, deep hole. Strangely, this hole transported them right back to school, to S12 (the science lab). There was a red button.

"Press it," said Harry.

Jaiden had already pressed it as Harry looked out of the window. He noticed the 'zombies' were all popping, disappearing, evaporating, dying.

Maybe everyone shouldn't always think the worst of these three boys, after all.

THE MYSTERIOUS BEACH

Emily Coe

1

Emily is an 11-year-old secondary school student. She has a lovely pale oval face with no imperfections – yet – with big brown eyes. Her hair is elbow length and light brown in colour. She always wears her favourite bright pink scrunchie in a ponytail, with a cheap digital Cassio watch on her left wrist.

Emily has come from a quiet, peaceful village, where everyone knows everybody, to a chaotic, loud, busy town with her family. She is a new Y7 student and is finding it hard to adjust to this new school. Whilst she is in the middle of a test, she can hear the constant tapping of the pens and pencils. This begins to irritate her and she struggles to concentrate.

Panicking, she leaves the room and all her things behind. She walks away in relief at getting out of that miserable, unbearable classroom.

After that, she goes on a wander to calm herself, doing her best to keep out of view from other students and teachers roaming the corridors. It does puzzle her that no one is chasing her after her sudden exit. Does no one care? Didn't anyone notice?

Before she starts to overthink the situation, she pushes open a large, wooden, heavy door, thinking it was the girl's toilet but in fact it was not…

Unexpectedly, she walks into an unknown and mysterious place. Looking around, she sees amazing sky-blue waves overlapping each other, one at a time, continuously. Her shoes begin to slowly sink into the crystal white sands beneath her feet. Blinded by the dazzling sun, she raises her hand up to her forehead to shield her eyes from the blinding sun. That's when she sees him.

Jack, an ancient man, has a cane in one

hand and a newspaper in the other, that looks like it has been read 100 times and is from the 1960s. He has a crooked body that is bent over double, his greying hair is thin and blows in the breeze, his clothes are dirty and dull in colour.

Emily slowly walks up to him and asks, "Who are you and where am I?"

Jack then replies with, "I am Jack and you have come to a beach through the floating door." His voice is croaky and rough.

Emily looks back and sees the mysterious floating door. Emily replies with, "Then why don't you open it?"

Jack looks at her for a long time and says, "You can't, you have to find the key and the resources before midnight."

"What happens if I don't get it before midnight?"

Jack sighs. "You get stuck here forever like me…"

2

Emily then begins to search for the treasure, even though she doesn't have a clue where to start (as Jack isn't much help). The beach first, she walks around for what feels like hours with no hope of success, but then she comes across a dark cave hidden amongst the cliffs. Nervously she wanders into the darkness, trying hard to focus her eyes into the pitch black, thinking to herself, "This is hopeless without a torch."

Losing hope, she realises there must be somewhere she hasn't searched, somewhere she must have missed. Then out of nowhere Jack's rough voice whispers, "You haven't searched one spot yet… the island!"

Confused, she spins to face him. "Island? What island?"

His crooked finger reaches out into the distance. Following his direction, she sees a faint Island lost into the great sea in front of her.

"How on earth do you expect me to get over there?" she asks incredulously.

"Use a boat!" Jack replies, with a smug smile.

Half hidden under sand and seaweed is what looks like a rowing boat. Tossing off the crabs and digging out the boat with her bare hands, more of the rowing boat emerges. Dragging it to the shoreline, she climbs in nervously. "Will this even float?"

Her question is not answered.

"Jack?"

He's vanished!

Finally, Emily makes it to the Island, tired and drenched from the seawater. All she wants to do is lay down on the sands and sleep — how long has it been since she went to bed? Before she can scare herself with a tonne of questions, she realises it's getting late, and she must hurry as soon her time will run out.

Suddenly, she notices hundreds of crabs surrounding a rundown, ancient green hut. She fights off the creatures with a wooden plank that lies in the sand. As Emily finally enters the hut, the only thing she finds is dust, cobwebs and the sickening smell of damp and lots more sand! Buried underneath all of it she finds a rusty metal detector.

Realising this stranger could be tricking her, as there is not much on this small wasteland of an island, Emily gives up her search and decides it's time to head back to find Jack. Rowing back frantically as the skies darken and the waves become bigger and stronger, she notices a cloth floating, so she brings the boat to a stop and retrieves it out of the now black water.

Once ashore, Emily runs ups to Jack who has now reappeared on the beach and is sitting there next to a roaring fire.

As the sand flicks up behind her, she shouts, "Jack, look what I've found! Do you think it will work?"

Jack and Emily clean the metal detector as best as they can. They try the switch, and it works!

"YES!" they both scream in delight.

3

The tide is slowly crawling up the sand towards the dying fire. The air is cold and chilly, stars begin to fill the skies and the sun has almost completely faded away. Emily and Jack are frantically running around the beach.

"There's nothing here!" Emily panics.

"There must be!" Jack croaks. "You must keep looking!"

Her eyes widen on the cave.

"Quick!" she yells. "Pass me that cloth!"

Wrapping the cloth around a stick tightly, she stabs the stick into the fire. Letting out sparks and a hiss, the cloth starts to burn. She makes her way to the cave, making sure not to set herself on fire.

As the droplets of water drip from the roof of the cave on to the fire, it lets out a creepy hissing sound.

"Be careful!" Jack shouts.

Rolling her eyes, Emily swaps hands and continues to look around the damp dull cave for anything that can help them. Suddenly, the light from the fire scares a sleeping bat that almost attacks Emily as it flies away. Screaming, Emily drops the fire torch. Luckily, it just misses a puddle of water by an inch.

"Whoa, that was close!" Emily exclaims.

Deeper into the cave Emily creeps, holding the fire torch lower as the roof of the cave starts to curve inwards.

"I don't like this, Jack," Emily says worriedly.

"Me neither, I've never gone this far into the cave, but we must keep going, it's almost midnight," Jack replies eagerly.

As they walk over the sharp spikey rocks, Emily notices an area of crystal white sand hidden away deeper in the cave.

Flicking the switch on the rusty metal detector, Emily is frustrated when it doesn't work.

"Try it again!" Jacks shouts impatiently.

Trying it again, the same happens, no power. Losing her temper, she slams the metal detector against a cold hard rock. Then suddenly, "Beep Beep, Beep Beep, Beep Beep!" echoes through the cave.

"Dig, dig!" Jack shouts excitedly.

Emily foolishly drops the torch to the floor and as the light slowly fades away, she digs frantically.

4

"I FOUND SOMETHING!" she bellows.

As Jack dashes over to where Emily is, he is met with complete darkness as the torch sizzles out.

"No, you idiot!" Jack screeches at Emily.

"It's okay. I'll find it" Emily says reassuringly.

"You best do. This is my only chance to get out of this miserable place," Jack snarls.

Shocked at how viciously he is speaking to her, Emily has a keen sense of dread and mistrust in him, so hides the small box she is holding into her blazer pocket.

As they crawl carefully over the rocks, their eyes squint desperately in need of some light.

"It's this way, I know it is!" Jack yells, pulling Emily by the sleeve.

She trembles at his command and follows him without saying a word.

In the deafening silence, they can hear the crashing of the waves against the rocks and cliffs outside. However, because it begins to echo through the cave, it makes it harder and more confusing to know which way they came.

Finally, moonlight begins to glisten off the water droplets on the cave walls, showing them the way out of the darkness and to safety.

"We made it, Jack!" Emily shouts excitedly.

"What did you find? Give it to me! I need to see it!" he demands.

Protecting her pocket, Emily exclaims abruptly, "Just you wait one second, what is wrong with you, Jack? We must work together if we BOTH want to get out of here!"

"I'm sorry, Emily, but I've been here for fifty years or more and I just want to see my family," Jack sobs.

5

Emily forgives him and says, "It's okay, just please stop snapping at me and let's work as a team. Anyway, let's get out of here!"

With that, Emily finally uncovers what she hid inside her blazer pocket. A rectangular, battered, rusty iron box with faded floral patterns, inside which lies an ancient large iron key.

Jack's eyes widen as wide as the smile that spreads across his face. "We've found it! Thank you so much, Emily!" he exclaims.

They run up to the large brown, heavy wooden door floating above the sand in the beautiful moonlight.

Emily glances down at the watch on her wrist. "It's 11:59, Jack. We made it!" she says with a smile on her face.

Placing the key into the rusty keyhole, they both take a deep breath and slowly twist the key. All they can hear is the clicks and clanks as the key is still turning.

Finally the turning stops and the large

door creaks open. Bright white light flashes through the crack, blinding them.

As Emily walks into the door, she can faintly hear the students' and teachers' voices getting louder and clearer until she can only just make out the school corridor.

Emily sprints further into the white light and exclaims, "Yes! We made it!" She looks back to help her new friend through the door but he's gone!

And so is the door.

"Jack! Jack!? Where are you? JACK!" She slowly starts sobbing. Did he make it? What could have happened? Where could he be?

6

"There you are, Emily," a soft voice says.

Still sobbing, she looks up and in her tearful eyes she sees a blurry figure standing over her. They reach out their hand and she grabs hold of it softly. They help her to her feet and then she realises the person in front of her is her teacher.

Her heart sinks.

"You're not Jack..." she whispers.

She slowly follows the teacher back to the classroom, not listening to a word being said, because all she can think about is poor Jack on the beach, dying alone. She doesn't notice the other children all around her or hear their mocking laughter at her tears. She silently sits down at her chair and lowers her head into her arms on her desk.

Then she remembers why she ran out of the classroom before.

Sniffing, she starts to focus on the whispers around her.

"She's a freak."

"She actually locked herself in a cupboard!"

"Look at her sitting in the corner by herself."

There are giggles.

Eventually, the whispers stop, and the room fills with silence.

That's when the chair beside her is dragged slowly out.

She refuses to look up from her desk.

Curiously, she gains the confidence to look up to whoever is sitting beside her, wiping the tears from her eyes. She sees a handsome young boy with brown hair.

Something is familiar about him.

He smiles beautifully at her and says, "Hi, my name's Jack."

The end… or is it?

INTO THE LIGHT
(A story for people suffering from anxiety)

Leoni Dixon

The classroom was busy, so busy that Lilly could not cope anymore. Her heart was pounding, her eyes watering and her nerves telling her to leave.

In the room, she could hear the constant chatter of students. Through the window, the weather was boiling hot. Lily left.

1: STUPID PROBLEMS…

It was a warm and sunny day. Lily had just finished her morning pancakes. She looked up to her mum, who had just finished doing the washing. She wanted to tell her about her stupid problems, but she was too scared. Lily's mum picked her bag up and pushed her out the door. Here she was again…her heart began to pound.

Finally, the school bus arrived. Lily hopped on and was greeted by Molly, her only friend who utterly understood her stupid problems. They got to school, and Lily was already walking into her class that she called "a waste of time." She sat at her desk and slumped back in her chair, breathing a sigh of frustration. Suddenly everyone started to chatter and scream in Lily's ear.

"Please stop it," she cried. At this point Lily felt invisible. Her eyes darted across the room, frantically trying to find a way to escape all the chatter. Out the corner of her eye, Lily saw an old oak door and a handle gently glowing to lure her in. Lily left the classroom. All was silent.

"What's this?" she asked herself, trying not to cry. Should she go in?

Yes, yes, she should.

2: OPEN THE DOOR

As Lily opened the door, she noticed a quick flash of light that made her feel unwelcome and afraid. Lily was confused. She saw a teen shouting at his parents, but his cries of frustration were lost on the breeze, and she could not hear the cause. She saw the rain pouring from the full clouds, but she could not hear the damp pitter patter on the concrete floor. How peculiar. Was Lily in a world without sound? Her dream world?

Yes, yes, she was.

What should she do first? So many sights and the sound made her feel free. The sound of nothing. She caught a glimpse of a short creature. He was strange, almost like a goblin. He was short and had a long shaggy beard. Lily's eyes widened. She had encountered a stubby goblin. He walked towards her leaving a trail of smell behind him. Lily was confused. The creature held up a piece of card and it read:

'Hello, do not be startled by me. I am Stinks the tree goblin. I will do you no harm. You need to help us. We are trapped in a land with no sound. We are all petrified. You need to save us, Lily. You must find the secret crystal hidden in this small town. Once you find it you will enable us to hear the rain and the wind. They are clues along the way. I will lead you to the first clue. Follow me.'

Lily wanted the ground to swallow her. She followed Stinks. He pointed to a green gate, an old rusty piece of metal. She could see pen marker on it.

It read: 'Hello child! Open this gate and you will begin your adventure to find the golden crystal to save us.'

She looked at Stinks and Stinks looked at her. He nodded politely.

Okay here goes nothing. She opened the gate.

Inside, there was an empty field with an eerie old house. Stinks led the way. She was ready to save this sacred town.

3: SAVING THE PEOPLE

Lily followed Stinks and looked down at her boots. They were full of mud. Her face turned green. Stinks was at the house which opened to another goblin, more appealing than Stinks. This goblin held up a long bit of paper and it read: 'Hello, Lily, come in'.

She walked up the steps onto the decking, trying to scrape the thickness of the mud off her boots before she stepped into the dark and damp house. Stinks pointed to the kitchen. Lily walked towards him, curious about what he had found. It was a spider, but not a spider you find in your garden. It was bright red, and it scurried across the kitchen floor. It ran out of the door. Lily knew it was a clue as it was different to the spiders at her home. She ran out, Stinks following her. The spider was in a hurry. Lily followed it closely.

Finally, the red spider came to a halt. Its body was on a strip of card on the grass.

Yes! Another clue!

It read: 'Look up!'. She did, and saw a huge hill standing above her.

She looked back at the card and read the last of the clue. 'Walk towards it and you will find a shovel, use it to dig the mud. There you will find the crystal'.

Lily thought that the clues were extremely easy, and she was so close to saving this town. Stinks ran with Lily to find the shovel.

4: LILY'S SAVE

Locating the large spade, Lily grabbed it with excitement. She put her thumb up to Stinks who was dancing with joy. She started to shovel the mud out of the hill. Hours passed and Lily was still there. Just as she was about to give up, her shovel hit something hard. She had found it - the golden crystal!

Laughter filled the air, even though you could not hear it. The goblin held a card up again: 'Let us return this to the goblin's house from earlier. She will restore the magic and we can hear again. As she gains the magic, you will disappear back to your town'.

Lily smiled. They walked back to the house. This time, Lily opened the door. It opened to a happy smiling face. She gave the crystal to the goblin. She held it in her cold hand. flexing her fingers. The crystal lit up and sound waves hit the air. The wind blew and you could hear it.

"Thank you, Lily," she replied with a breathtaking hug and Lily softly replied, "You're welcome!" and she started to fade.

5: HOMEBOUND

Lily was back at her usual desk. She was home. The kids still chattered around her, but she was okay with that.

She sat back in her chair as if nothing had happened. Surprisingly, her heart was at a steady beat. She felt calm. Wow. Lily was relaxed. She'd forgotten that she could experience relaxation.

Later, that day she returned home.

"How was school love?" her mum asked, expecting her to say how awful it was, instead she replied with, "It was amazing!" Her mum was confused, but she went with it. Lily smirked and said, "I'll tell you later." Lily's mum shrugged her shoulders and carried on with her washing.

Lily paused and then asked, "Mum, have you ever experienced life with no sound?"

Her mum paused her washing and said, almost whispering, "Yes, when I was your age, I went through a strange door, and it led me to a world without sound."

Lily's mum paused and opened her mouth, but it closed again. "But I was young. I must have imagined it all. Why are you asking, Lily?"

"I don't know just curious, must have been a bad dream, mum."

Mum turned away and carried on with her washing.

"Mum, it was not a dream."

Lily's stupid problems were solved. Later that night, she sat in her bed, smiling at the thought that Stinks was now happy. "I will see you again, Stinks, I promise." She crossed her fingers and held them up to her bedroom ceiling.

Lily's problems are now solved. Now, go and solve yours.

THE MYSTERIOUS STORM

H.J. Hakin

In the dark corridor at 7.30am as Jack went to get his clothes for the day ahead, looking out of the window, he saw a terrible storm… he did not fancy going to school in the rain.

Peeking through his mother's bedroom door, Jack saw no one there – the bed had not been slept in. He went downstairs to check if his father was there. He was not. His room was empty, no movement, no nothing. Jack was then confused.

He went to check the time. It had reached 7.50.

By the time he had unlocked his phone, he heard a noise downstairs, so he went to investigate. There was nothing there, but the power had cut out.

Jack was extremely nervous. Thinking that he needed to find some normality –

even though he hated the place – Jack ran to school.

Speeding towards school, his stomach tensed with dread. Every day, the same boys made his life a misery and now a mysterious storm had turned his world upside down.

Arriving at school, he checked the time. It was 9.00. School should have started by now. He was cold, nervous, and worried.

As soon as Jack entered the school door, he quickly realised that this was not normal… all the windows were boarded up, there was no noise, no lights, no power. As he carefully moved around the school, he started to hear a noise.

It was a very strange noise… he could not think about anything else.

Then Jack heard footsteps… it was someone he knew. Well, at least he thought that. She had curly brown hair and cruel blue eyes that had taunted and mocked him every day. Strange though, she had not replied when he said, "Hello."

Jack decided to just keep walking though

his skin tingled with suspicion. Hearing banging and crashing noises, Jack ran into a classroom and looked outside the window.

The storm was getting worse. The wind picked up fences and started to blow them into the Sports Centre which was in the other playground. The windows started to smash. Jack soon had to hide under the tables to avoid flying glass.

The table under which he was taking shelter tipped over with the wind. He had no cover now.

He tried to open the door but again, he failed. He thought only option was to use the window that had smashed, until he saw Angela beckoning him through the classroom door.

Terrified, Jack moved towards her.

"If we work together, we can get out of here!" she shouted.

Jack was confused. He was not used to Angela being kind to him at all. It was like she was a different person. It really seemed as though she wanted to help him. They battled down the stairs, shouting to each other to avoid anything flying through the air.

Angela pulled him round a corner and for a moment there was calm.

"I thought you hated me," Jack said, breathing heavily.

Angela smiled at him and put her hand on his shoulder. "I'm sorry, Jack. It was the only way I could think of to stop other people making my life a misery. If they were out to get you… they might leave me alone."

The storm raging outside the windows seemed to calm.

"How about from now on," Jack said, "we try being friends?"

As Angela nodded, the strange school door unlocked with a click.

Jack headed back through that door. The sun was shining.

Crowds of students were heading towards the school, which was just as it was on any normal day. His phone pinged with a text message from his Mum – since there was such nice weather, they'd have a barbeque that evening.

Just then, a group of students run past him, pushing into him. One of them stopped and turned. It was Angela.

"Sorry!" she shouted, and winked at him.

Jack smiled.

THE SCHOOL MYSTERY

Summer Loftus

It was a cold wintery morning at Laurence Jackson School. Everyone was trying to get through all the hustle and bustle of the late students. The corridors were full of shouting, screaming, and pushing.

1: BEING LATE

Emily was getting pushed about with all the hustle and bustle. She was often late to class – she had very few friends and nobody would want or even offer to show her around. Suddenly, she realised that she had forgotten where and what class she was supposed to be in. She frantically tried to remember the time as she got closer to being late – again. She decided to check every classroom in the school. Finally, she saw what her classroom could be, and she remembered – it was drama. Her worst nightmare.

2: THE UNUSUAL DRAMA CLASS

As Emily glared at the classroom door – which looked different to how she remembered – she thought herself, 'What if it isn't my class? What if they all laugh at me?'

She felt sick to her stomach that she would find out that it was not her class, and she would get in trouble. She took another long glare at the door. Pushing the strange door slightly, she suddenly began to feel like her heart was going to beat out of her chest.

3: WILL EMILY KNOCK ON THE DOOR?

Emily knocked on the door and entered.

The whole class fell silent. There was no teacher in sight.

Emily began to ask herself why the students were wearing their own clothes and why there were no sheets or books on the desk, but someone was playing loud music and it was booming out of control.

Emily tapped one girl on the shoulder and asked her name.

"Sophie," she replied.

4: MY CLASS

Emily was sure she had not heard the name before.

Sophie spoke to Emily unlike all the other students. "What year are you in?" she asked kindly.

Emily replied that she was in Year 7 and

Sophie asked her to take her timetable from her bag.

Sophie was in the same year as Emily, so she offered to help and took Emily to her class.

5: WILL EMILY AND SOPHIE BECOME FRIENDS?

As they walked through the corridors, Emily began to talk to Sophie. The panic that had been in her chest before now was disappearing, slowly. They became friends because they found out that they had so much in common – same favourite food, same movie, same lessons in school.

As Sophie pointed out Emily's classroom door, she reached out to push it, looking back at her new friend. But Sophie had started to disappear, fading as the door creaked open.

Full of panic, Emily stepped into the classroom. Her classmates were sitting completing a bell task. The teacher smiled at her and showed her where to sit.

The girl – in uniform – sitting next to her space looked up.

It was Sophie!

Emily smiled at her and knew that school was never going to be so frightening again.

THE FLOWER

Tulisa Lowe

The room was dark. She could hear someone but did not know who it was.

"Tulisa!"

She heard her name but could not see anyone. She stayed still and did not say a word, closing her eyes and whispering to herself, "Whoever you are, don't hurt me!"

Tulisa closed her eyes slowly.

"Don't be scared, Tulisa."

She heard a warm softening voice behind her. She turned around.

"Tulisa, it's okay. Don't worry, it's just a test," whispered Miss Dear.

She opened her eyes and recognised where she was.

"You can go outside and have a breather."

Tulisa stepped outside and closed her eyes, took three deep breaths, and opened them again. She looked up at the old, stale wall and, looking down, saw something – a door with a gold handle and paint peeling off it. Looking around, she touched the glistening handle and gently pulled it. Taking a deep breath, she hesitantly put her foot out and closed her eyes; she felt like she was floating, and her tummy knotted up.

Peeking through her eyelashes, she saw a faint little figure with a wide, clumsy stance. He had a long, ragged, knotted beard. She had never seen a man so small and grumpy from his facial expression.

Her eyes widened in shock, with her jaw on the floor.

"Someone's here! I can't believe it. Someone's here!" shouted the small grubby man. "Who are you? Hello, I am taking to you!

"I am Tulisa," she said in scared voice.

"Well, I am Tinkle Tiny."

"Tinkle Tiny?" said a confused Tulisa.

"Yes, I am here to help you."

"With what?" replied Tulisa.

"Your fear, of course!" said Tinkle Tiny.

Though the situation was confusing,

Tulisa recognised the problem the strange creature was talking about.

However, she had no time to think about it as suddenly - as quick as thunder, her fear overtook her and she started to breathe faster and faster. She wanted to scream but she did not have a voice to do it with.

An unknown person hugged her tightly and said, "It's okay, my dearest friend. I am here."

She opened her eyes slowly to be greeted by a girl she did not know who spoke gently. "I know I am a stranger, and you don't know me, but it looked like you needed some help."

Through a dry throat, Tulisa whispered, "Thank you."

Before she could blink, the girl was gone and Tinkle Tiny reappeared, saying, "We best be off!"

"Where?"

"To find the flower, of course – to make your problems go away!"

Tulisa was confused but worried that she

would not make it in time before she had another attack.

"Come on!" shouted Tinkle Tiny.

They headed into a dense forest, pushing through many obstacles which Tinkle Tiny, with his humour, helped her to overcome. Finally, they made it to the flower. It glowed as soon as they saw it.

In shock, Tulisa slowly picked up the flower up and, under Tinkle Tiny's instruction, placed it in her pocket.

Walking and talking together, the pair were soon back at the door through which Tulisa had entered the strange world, and near the entrance was a girl.

"Wait!" said Tulisa in an excited voice. "She helped me, let me go say hello!"

She walked over to the girl and hugged her.

The girl's eyes filled with tears and she fell to the ground.

"It's okay," Tulisa said, "I am here."

Tulisa looked at the girl who seemed like she was about to pass out and then felt the velvety petals of the flower in her pocket.

She thought to herself, 'She needs it more than me.'

As Tulisa placed the flower in the girl's hand, a million shots of light illuminated the sky. The girl's breathing became slower and her tears stared to dry.

She stood up and smiled, saying, "Thank you so much. My name is Lily, by the way. I must go now, but I will repay you when I can."

Tulisa smiled and said, "No need to repay me because I am repaying you!"

The girl smiled and walked away slowly.

Tinkle Tiny asked her why she had given away the previous flower.

"Always help someone in need," Tulisa smiled.

"But you need that flower too!" Tinkle Tiny said in disbelief.

"She needed it more."

Tulisa walked back to the door and opened it, walking back into the classroom as if she'd never left. She didn't feel scared anymore.

VERDUN!

Oliver Morris

1: WELCOME TO MY LIFE!

There was a shooting in a bar in Joseph's home country. He didn't like to think about, remember it or talk about it but it meant that he was all alone and was sent to a boarding school in Winchester, Hampshire. He hated school, as did his one friend, Elijah Turner. Elijah was the only person who noticed Joseph in lessons. Joseph noticed almost nothing.

On the day in question, his first lesson was History – his least skilful subject. Desperate for the lesson to pass, he stared at the board and saw multiple posters about World War 1, 'Tanktastic Victory at Verdun!' with pictures of huge armoured vehicles below them. Elijah was muttering something about his great-grandfather,

Captain Jack Turner, but even that couldn't interest Joseph.

The teacher announced a test later on in the lesson. Joseph was so bored, he asked to go to the toilet – planning to stay there as long as possible.

As soon as Mr Jones, his teacher, said, "Yes," Joseph bolted out of the door, not even realising it had changed and was far from the modern, double-glazed entrance he was used to.

2: WELCOME TO HELL!

As Joseph walked through the old wooden door, he immediately saw a wall of mud with small grooves all over. He was bewildered. Looking around, he saw he was in fact surrounded by mud – the door had disappeared. He was terrified and disorientated.

As he went to reach for it, his phone vanished from his blazer pocket. All he could hear was shouting, loud bangs, whizzing zips. He could smell something metallic and more of a rotten smell. It. Was. Horrible.

He saw multiple men run past, all wearing bowl-like helmets, brown uniforms and webbing pouches. They were all dark khaki in colour and carrying canteens of water. But then one stopped in his tracks. His hat looked different to the others as did his uniform. He called out, "Hey kid, who are you and why are you here?"

Joseph replied, "I don't even know where I am, let alone why I'm here!"

"I am Commander Jack Turner of the 34th Expeditionary Corps. And you?"

Joseph hesitated – the name sounded familiar – but eventually he replied, "I'm Joseph and I'm a student at Winchester Boarding School."

The commander looked shocked at how a school boy had made it to the trenches and asked, "Do you know where you are?"

Joseph shook his head.

"You are in Verdun, 1916, in the War to end all Wars!" he smiled.

Joseph was terrified – he didn't know much

about history but he knew that Verdun was like the Somme. It was a bloody battle to last the ages.

3: THE BATTLE!

He now knew what that whizzing noise was… it was bullets! And those loud bangs, they were explosions! He had gone through the door, to escape Mr Jones' history lesson and had inadvertently travelled 107 years into the past! He was too stunned to speak.

"Oi! Kid! What was your name… Oh yeah, Joseph!" The commander yelled until Joseph finally answered.

"I need to get back to 2023!"

"2023?! Are you insane?" the commander replied in an incredulous tone.

"No! I came here through a door that's disappeared!"

The commander finally came to terms after a minute of arguing which was interrupted by a loud explosion almost deafening the soldiers nearby.

"Kid, we need help winning this battle. You're from the future – what do we do?"

Joseph's mind was blank – like it was most of the time he was at school – but he paused and remembered the image on his classroom wall under the title 'Tanktastic Victory at Verdun!'

"Use tanks!" he said like he knew everything.

"Tanks?" the commander said. "You mean those metal boxes? Can't move very fast?"

"USE THEM!" Joseph yelled.

"Fine! You don't have to yell. Get me the carrier pigeon! Its name is Jeff, I believe."

Joseph ran as if thousands of lives were in his hands - which they were. He grabbed Jeff's cage and ran back to the commander who was ducking and writing a note that said 'GET THOSE TANKS HERE NOW!' The commander took Jeff, wrapped the note round his leg and let him fly towards friendly lines. It was turning dark, this meant German trench raiders – a living nightmare!

4: THE NIGHTMARE COMES TO LIFE!

The American and British troops were awake all night – waiting. Joseph tried to sleep but all he could think about was school. He longed for the safety of desks and textbooks full of facts. This was a real shock to him as he hated being in a classroom. He was thinking even a strict boarding school like Winchester was better than almost dying every day.

At midnight, he was woken up by the commander. "Come on, kid, tanks have arrived, we can raid the Fritz!"

"Really? This could be my way back!" Joseph said excitedly.

"Take this…" The commander gave him a bowl helmet.

As Joseph looked at the label on the hat's inner surface, he heard his friend Elijah's voice… "My great grandfather…"

"Safety!" the commander said.

Later in the evening – 12.30 to be exact – he was in a tank with the commander and his men.

"Alright lads, let's get him home," he said.

As they moved through the German trench, Joseph saw the door, shimmering slightly to their left. He walked towards it, but was stopped by the commandant of the Germans. His name was on his dog tags: 'C. Hans Schuller'.

"Where do you think you're going?" He spoke in a heavy accent.

"Home!" Joseph said bravely – the commandant laughed and charged at them. Joseph ducked, went through his legs and back through the door.

Back in the classroom, he thought perhaps he'd been in a fever dream. He saw some rubble on his shoulder, and his foot knocked against the metal of the Captain's helmet below his desk. Mr Jones asked a question about Verdun. Joseph smiled.

Maybe History wasn't so bad after all.

BECOMING MIO

Kai Watson

"Agh…" Mio stared forward at the boy.

It was a bright, sunny day – almost too hot. The classroom was a mess, cooking supplies everywhere. The noise of banging pots and whisks filled the air whilst the smell of cake burning floated up from the oven.

Feeling overwhelmed, Mio headed towards the plain panelled wooden door to leave. However, a few moments later, she had turned back around to face the door. Weirdly, the wooden panels had changed to a bunch of tiny repeating mosaic tiles…

She shrugged it off, heading back through it and closed her eyes. As Mio opened her eyes, she looked forward into the silent classroom.

A quill scratched off the paper.

She smelt the air, the smell of stale ink.

She stared forward at a quill, the scratching of it the only noise in the silent classroom. Next, she turned her head to the person, a boy from her class, his name was Benjamin.

Benjamin's black, scruffy hair had stayed, just his clothes changed. Mio stared down at what he was wearing, a button up overcoat, midnight black with tailored trousers.

As silence filled the classroom again, she looked down at her own clothes, her jeans and jumper had been replaced by a floor-length dress fitted to her narrow waist, her breath struggling against a skin-tight corset. Mio quickly looked back up at the boy as she had felt his eyes on her but, he was back to doing his work.

Mio looked over again, spotting a window and staring at her vivid reflection. The reflection was as clear as a photographic image or perhaps a mirror. Her brown, tangled hair covering her eyes, she began to brush it out of her face, intrigued by the detail she could see before her.

When she looked back up, she looked to the front, where a chalkboard stood tall, as if it was guarding some sort of property. She continued to stare, trying to work out what was written on it, but she jumped as the floor creaked and the man at the front of the classroom turned round to stare right back at her.

She smiled awkwardly as the man walked to the back towards her. He glared at her, walking towards her slowly, then looking her up and down before finally settling approximately one metre away from her.

"Why aren't you sitting down?" a broad, deep voice, bellowed.

She felt the whole room stare at her. Mio stared back. She tried to speak, her voice breaking at every word – nothing would come out.

The man tapped his foot, speaking once again. "No excuse? Right then, sit up straight before there's a consequence."

Looking around, she realised everyone had turned round, then looked at the same boy again. She quickly rushed to a bench as the teacher reached the front, grabbing a quill and resting it above the paper. She stared at the person's paper, copying it all down as quickly as she could.

The man placed down his chalk. A bell was ringing – was it the end of the day or just a break?

Mio stared outside. She stood up after all the others, placing her quill down then taking the paper to the front for the demanding man.

Following all the others outside, she tried to catch up with Benjamin, but she got pushed back, being led to a playground full of girls. She slumped down on a bench; all the girls were playing with these dumb hoops. She walked down the steps, staring into the boy's playground. She was about to violently vomit. Football, a normal kids' game but they were playing it with a pig's stomach!

Mio stared forward, then around her... there were no teachers. As she started walking up to the boy's area, thoughts flooded her head – what if I get caught? Am I really doing this? What am I thinking? I need to do this – I need to find out why we're all here. She walked forward, into the boy's area.

Tapping Benjamin on the shoulder, he jumped.

"Huh...?!" His voice was mid-tone and tinged with panic.

"Be quiet!" Mio whispered loudly, her voice bossy. She grabbed hold of Benjamin's hand and dragged him away, out of the boys' area and round a nearby corner.

"GET OFF!" Benjamin shouted at her.

Mio quickly covered her ears out of fear.

"Calm down!" she shouted back. "Anyway, I brought you here for one thing, I need to ask you something." Mio's tone went back to normal, her same high-pitched, soft voice.

"Get on with it then."

"Alright, calm down. Why are we all here? I was in the cooking room then I come out and I'm here!"

"Like I would know! I just ended up here after you left the room."

Mio started picking repeatedly at her nails, especially her cuticles. She then turned around, about to walk off as Benjamin grabbed her shoulder.

"Wait, I know maybe. You need to get over your anxiety and calm down, stand up for yourself maybe. This all happened because of your anxiety and being overwhelmed."

Mio turned around and just nodded along. As they heard another bell ring, they ran to line up in their yards.

As they walked back into the classroom, Mio sat down next to Benjamin. As they started whispering, the teacher suddenly shouted with a booming volume that resonated through the room and everything in it.

"There will be no talking in my class!"

They both shrugged it off and continued to speak anyway. The consequence – the teacher reached down, grabbing his cane.

"Be quiet!" he boomed once again.

Mio looked at Benjamin and as they met each other's stare, both bursting out laughing. They both closed their eyes.

Opening them again, Mio stared forward, catching sight of Benjamin back in the cooking classroom. Both of their faces lit up as Mio returned to her station to finish the school day.

The end... or is it?